Theodore Francis Green

The Washington Years

Theodore Francis Green

Theodore Francis Green

The Washington Years, 1937–1960

ERWIN L. LEVINE

Brown University Press · Providence

International Standard Book Number: 0–87057–126–5
Library of Congress Catalog Card Number: 73–127366
Brown University Press, Providence, Rhode Island 02912
Published 1971
Printed in the United States of America
By Connecticut Printers, Inc.
On Warren's Olde Style
Bound by Stanhope Bindery
Designed by Richard Hendel

IN MEMORY OF

SINCLAIR ARMSTRONG

JAMES BLAINE HEDGES

MATTHEW MITCHELL

Contents

Preface

THEODORE FRANCIS GREEN (1867–1966) was a United States senator from Rhode Island from 1937 through 1960. A devoted adherent of the Democratic party, from 1933 to 1937 he served two consecutive terms as governor of the nation's smallest state (for his political career prior to 1937 see Erwin L. Levine, *Theodore Francis Green: The Rhode Island Years, 1906–1936.* Providence, 1963). Green first went to the Senate in 1937 during the height of New Deal fervor. In the latter part of Franklin D. Roosevelt's first term as president the United States Supreme Court had cast a disapproving eye on several New Deal measures, but the president began his second term bolstered by his landslide victory of November 1936. Green was a patrician Rhode Islander who thoroughly agreed with FDR's political pragmatism and with his social and economic philosophy. As governor of Rhode Island, Green had personified the progressive outlook of Roosevelt's New Deal program, and he looked upon his own election to the Senate in 1936 as justification for continuing to support the president in Washington.

Green purposely linked his own political beliefs with those of the president. He was able to establish political rapport with the same coalition of forces to which Roosevelt so easily appealed. When, for example, Green explained the intent and method of the social security system to the workers of Rhode Island, they listened with respect and responded with their votes, yet never felt that this elderly aristocrat who loved democracy with a passion was patronizing them. Nor did they ever forget that he had deep roots in early America and that his life exemplified the humanitarian, liberal, and progressive strain that has always been part of the American character. Theodore Francis Green was certain of the legitimacy of the liberal and progressive way of life. He believed that the less fortunate in society were entitled to governmental aid and political protection from oppressors. His political philosophy, in short, coincided with Roosevelt's but did not imitate it. Those who elected Green on six different occasions despite his age respected and admired him for his views, not because they saw in him the alter ego of FDR.

During Green's four terms in Washington the nation underwent significant changes in its national direction, as it experienced the social and economic ramifications of the New Deal and World War II, and the insecurity and uncertainty of the cold war. The nation emerged from isolationism to internationalism and became increasingly aware of its own inadequacies in the field of civil rights and social justice. Throughout these turbulent years, Green's political activities were grounded in his New Deal liberalism.

The scholar is fortunate when he is able to study sources that not only supply him with information relevant to his work but also broaden his view of the American political process. The extensive collection of his private papers that Senator Green gave to the Library of Congress at the conclusion of his tenure in the Senate proved to be more than just excellent raw material for the political examination of an individual senator. The years from 1937 to 1961 are a fertile period for political research, and far more was learned and assimilated than can ever be put into a single volume.

I am indebted to many people for easing the burdens of research. A number of those who granted interviews preferred not to be quoted directly, and I have of course followed their wishes.

My gratitude in particular goes to Senators John O. Pastore, Claiborne Pell, J. William Fulbright, John Sparkman, Bourke Hickenlooper, and the late Everett Dirksen. Among many Senate professional staff members, I wish to thank Gordon Harrison, Robert Dunphy, James McKenna, Ray Nelson, Paul Goulding,

Carl Marcy, Pat Holt, Orlando Potter, Morella Hansen, Ruth Bamber, and Lee Szilagy. Frederick Bernays Wiener, Washington attorney and long a friend of Senator Green, offered much advice, and to him I am especially grateful. I am also indebted to Caroline C. Cornwell and Elmer E. Cornwell, Jr.

I can never fully express my appreciation to Edward J. Higgins, citizen of Rhode Island and the most democratic of Democrats. If anyone has taught me the need to understand the art of politics, it is Mr. Higgins, who granted me numerous interviews as well as access to his private papers.

I would also like to acknowledge the assistance of Barbara Smith and Alvin Skipsna of the Skidmore College library staff and that of Miss Susan Weale, my student assistant at Skidmore College.

Finally, I am deeply grateful to the Howard Foundation, Brown University, and Skidmore College for financial support.

Theodore Francis Green

The Washington Years

1. President's Man

THEODORE FRANCIS GREEN made his Washington debut as the freshman junior senator from Rhode Island in January 1937. Having just won the greatest presidential victory in history, with Green's support, Franklin D. Roosevelt dropped his Court reform bombshell shortly after his second-term inauguration. Senator Green thus began his career as a national legislator faced with the necessity of choosing sides in the most bitterly divisive fight yet provoked by his old friend and political idol.

There was never actually any question which side Green would support. He was personally devoted to FDR, he was a thoroughgoing New Dealer, as his two terms as governor of Rhode Island had shown, and after all, he had once packed a court himself. (Two years earlier he and his close advisors had engineered the replacement of the entire membership of the Rhode Island Supreme Court in what many angrily called a Latin American *coup d'état*.) Thus, all his instincts and impulses placed him squarely in the forefront of the president's none-too-numerous band of supporters.

The story of the so-called Court-packing plan need not be retold here. It is enough to recall that Roosevelt had become more and more concerned as he watched the Court strike down key New Deal statutes during his first term. A bloc of four archconservatives, joined by one of the two "swing" members of the bench, Chief Justice Charles Evans Hughes or Associate Justice Owen J. Roberts, often spelled doom for a challenged policy. The president, ill-advisedly, most agreed afterward, deviously planned legislation that would allow him to appoint a new justice for each member with ten years service still on the Court six months after his seventieth birthday—up to an over-all Court total of fifteen.

The Senate Republicans opposed the scheme unanimously. Although many Democrats viewed Roosevelt's plan with misgivings or open hostility, Green thrust himself into the fray on behalf of the White House. In a letter to the *New York Times* barely a month after taking office, he pointed out that the most vociferous opposition to the plan was emanating from those "whose theory of government [had been] overwhelmingly repudiated by the people at the last election." He went on to recall that bare majorities of the Court had been ignoring the will of the American people and of congressional majorities.[1]

In a nationwide radio speech broadcast two weeks later, Green elaborated on the president's proposal.[2] Describing himself as a conservative New Englander with deep respect for tradition, Green demanded immediate reform. In making his case for the plan, he carefully evaded polemics concerning the age of the justices, the strongest argument for the Roosevelt proposal, since the most liberal man on the Court was Louis Brandeis, then eighty, and Green himself was almost seventy. In his speech Green drew attention to Roosevelt's basic respect for the Court and its personnel, pointing out that FDR, unlike some of his predecessors, had not defied the judges outright when their decisions were displeasing. In short, Green recapitulated the arguments of the president and his supporters for reform.

Green's stand, however, was not popular with many Rhode Islanders. His first attempt at shaping national policy brought sharp repercussions, demonstrating that many are quick to condemn, even when a senator supports as popular a president as Roosevelt, and proving that America has no tradition sanctifying loyalty to national party leaders. Correspondents called Roosevelt a dictator and expressed amazement that Green could possibly back such a man. Mrs. John Nicholas Brown (Natalie Dresser Brown), a prominent Rhode Islander who had supported his candidacy, telegraphed Green that his advocacy of the plan shocked his friends and might well destroy their confidence in his judgment and ability. This wire launched a lengthy exchange in which the senator tried to rebut the charges made against the president and then to answer new thrusts from his former patroness.[3]

Not all the opposition on this issue was from individuals. A large group of Rhode Island citizens, having formed the Emergency Committee of Rhode Island in order to combat the proposal, sent Green a petition urging him and the whole Rhode Island delegation to oppose the measure when it emerged from the Senate Judiciary Committee. Green's answer was to ask for the addresses of the 2,500 people whose names appeared on the petition. He wanted to have the signatories positively identified. He also wanted to put his case to the signatories, for along with most of the other newspapers in the country, Rhode Island newspapers had been opposing the president and the senator on this issue, so the case for the policy had to be made by other means than through the press. Green therefore sent each signer a brief memorandum setting forth his position.[4]

His public advocacy of the Court proposal continued unabated. In mid-March 1937 he received resolutions passed by the General Assembly in Providence on the controversial plan. The Democratic Rhode Island House of Representatives endorsed the president's proposal, while the Senate Republican majority took the opposite stand. In presenting these resolutions to the U.S. Senate Green took the opportunity to attack the position that the proposed Court reform should be accomplished by constitutional amendment rather than by simple act of Congress. The former method, he insisted, would leave the matter in the hands of unrepresentative state legislative houses like the Rhode Island Senate.[5]

In April, when the liberal justices were joined by Hughes and Roberts in upholding the National Labor Relations Act, the junior senator pointed out the undesirability of reliance on shifts of position by a single justice. The same month he addressed the Law Society of Massachusetts with another full-scale defense of the president's plan and blasted its opponents in a speech to the National Lawyers Guild in New York. These rhetorical efforts were carefully prepared because they were aimed at important, but hostile, audiences and would garner national coverage. In New York Green underscored his support of the proposal by arguing that there was "no other practical way of carrying out the principles of the New Deal, coming to the relief of a distraught people, and remedying the ills of our social and economic systems. . . ."[6]

The senator's office continued to receive communications showing the rising tide of public opposition, some of them from Green's most respected constituents. His former political advisor, the staunch academic advocate of free speech Zechariah Chafee, denounced the plan as an insult to the judiciary and an attempt to manipulate it politically.[7] Criticism by persons of such stature apparently prompted Green and his staff to do considerable research on the whole question, for there are several memoranda among his private papers that obviously had been used in public and private discussions of the issue. In one it is argued that the four conservatives on the Court were reactionary on questions of civil rights and civil liberties as well as on New Deal economic questions, that they had voted against the Wagner Act and mortgage relief legislation, but for the Texas white primary and a Minnesota press censorship law. This careful effort to link economic conservatism with conservatism on personal liberty and related issues suggests the subtlety and thoroughness which Green put into his self-chosen role as the president's champion.

Nothing, however, could stem the rising wave of opposition against the Court-packing plan. As students of the period know, Chief Justice Hughes's adroit defense of the Court and its record in a letter to Senator Burton K. Wheeler helped doom the administration's hopes for favorable action. The most tragic reversal was the death of Senator Joseph T. Robinson of Arkansas, who had gallantly led the fight as majority leader in spite of private reservations (perhaps, or so it is rumored, in exchange for a promise of the first vacancy on the reformed Court). This blow to the president's forces was accompanied by the resignation of Justice Willis Van Devanter, thus providing the president with a vacancy to fill, belying his argument that the reactionaries were permanently entrenched, and reducing their number to three.

The Court reorganization bill was killed by recommittal to the Senate Judiciary Committee on 22 July 1937. Green was one of twenty senators who voted against recommittal, and the following day the president commented that "you and I have had to keep trying for objectives many times in the past, even though we did not at first succeed. Judicial reform is coming, just as sure as God made little apples."[8] A week later Senator Green joined Roosevelt for a short cruise on the presidential yacht *Potomac*.

Precipitate involvement in the Court-packing struggle during his first six months as senator not only dramatically launched Green's new career but also set the style and provided the theme for his whole period in office. In his quiet way Green came to epitomize the loyal, dependable northern Democrat. Moreover, he evinced a loyalty to President Roosevelt and his programs—later largely transferred to President Truman—that was at least unusual, if not unique, in a congressman or senator. Although he shared Woodrow Wilson's international outlook, there is no evidence that Green shared Wilson's special admiration for the British political system; nevertheless, the role he chose for himself as senator came closer to that of the loyal parliamentary party member than is usually the case on Capitol Hill.

From the beginning of his involvement in Rhode Island politics, Green had taken a liberal Democratic line, in part because of his admiration of Wilson, but in greater part because of his total agreement with Roosevelt's New Deal. As governor, Green strove at the state level to support FDR's policies and to secure enactment of what amounted to a little New Deal.[9] Beyond this, however, Green had acquired from intellectual ancestors such as Thomas Wilson Dorr a deep personal commitment to democratic and humanitarian political ideals. This combination of influences made it inevitable that he would go to Washington a dedicated supporter of the Roosevelt administration.

The extent to which he was willing to adopt the role of "president's man" in the Senate belied to some extent the normal pattern of priorities common on Capitol Hill. Textbooks and scholarly literature frequently emphasize the dependence of the American legislator on his constituents; his loyalty to party, to the chief executive, or to any claimant for his allegiance beyond the boundaries of his district must yield to this, for his career and its future security ultimately stem from his constituents. Even when a safe district confers relative independence from home demands on the congressman, rarely does he use this freedom to tie himself voluntarily to the White House. More often he uses it to support special ideological or regional causes. Green, however, saw his proper role differently.

Even a senator with Green's bent, unlike a member of Parliament, must play other roles besides that of supporter of executive policies. Congress is a legislature in a fuller sense of that term than are the national assemblies of most democracies. Rather than merely ratifying executive proposals, it makes laws, and its members initiate proposals, even majority members often doing so without the blessing of their own party leadership. Thus, the role of legislator in Congress is separate from the role of either loyal party member or executive supporter. Robert F. Wagner, Sr., and George Norris made brilliant careers as legislative innovators. Green left no such dazzling record but did, nonetheless, play the role of legislator at a more modest level.

Under the conditions that prevail in the American legislative system, a congressman or senator must also be a representative as members of European parliaments rarely are. The latter, though elected nominally from districts, are answerable to parties or to powerful organized interests and thus represent their constituents only partially and indirectly. In the United States, on the other hand, constituents have the major claim on the loyalty of their representatives. Green understood this but tried nevertheless to see national issues as national issues even when home pressures dictated a more parochial view. But when questions arose that affected home industries or interests in which his concern was continuing, he played the representative role with skill, persistence, and considerable success.

A senator is also inescapably a politician. Having survived long immersion in the vigorous, even vicious, politics of Rhode Island before coming to Washington, Green knew the game and how to play it. So did his aide and confidant, Edward J. Higgins, who, having served at Green's right hand when he was governor of Rhode Island, came with him to Washington as his chief assistant. Between them they let little slip through their fingers in the way of patronage for supporters or benefits for their state. When it came to the party politics of Rhode Island, Green and Higgins maintained a far closer involvement than is typical of a congressional delegation.

Finally, a senator has a role to play within the institution of which he is a part. Students of Congress, and of the Senate in particular, have noted the informal establishment or inner-club aspects of that body. There is, for instance, the committee system, in which the individual climbs up the ladder until he inherits a chairmanship, whereupon his years of accumulating both seniority and expertise in a particular field accord him a position of semifeudal power that is unique in the American legislative system. Senator Green's involvement in this pattern of relationships must also be sketched, as well as his role in the special issues that came before the Senate during his tenure, among them those of the McCarthy censure and civil rights.

Green played all these roles. In none was he truly outstanding, save possibly that of faithful presidential supporter. In none did he attract widespread attention. He was not a brilliant legislator or innovator like Robert Wagner or George Norris. Nor was he an Arthur Vandenberg or a William Fulbright in foreign policy, an Ellison ("Cotton Ed") Smith in his dogged protection of home interests, or, least of all, a strident maverick like William Borah or Wayne Morse. Green's career was more typical, though less spectacular. In a sense this makes it all the more worthy of examination. If the Senate needs its Aldriches, Lodges, Byrds, and Kennedys, it also cannot dispense with its solid workmanlike members. If all senators strove for national reputations, too few would be left to do the day-to-day legislating, representing, and politicking.

Representatives in the Green tradition are the backbone of any legislative institution, even one like the United States Senate, in which members are so often tempted to strive for national plaudits, higher office, or the notoriety of rugged independence. Perhaps the Senate is especially in need of men like Green, of whose tenure in the Senate this study attempts to present a rounded, role-by-role picture. The essential ingredient of success in American legislatures may well be the ability to play simultaneously the half dozen or more separate roles that such office demands, roles that clash as often as they overlap and that require constant shifts of attention as well as subtle judgments. Green mastered this art. If he cannot be listed among the great members of Congress, he was certainly a senator of "usefulness and reputation," to borrow a phrase from the charter of his alma mater, Brown University.

Although Senator Green was on the losing side in the Court fight, the experience confirmed his determination to support President Roosevelt without stint, even in the face of hostile reaction at home. During those early months Green began to develop a reputation as an outspoken freshman that belied both his quiet, courteous manner and his age. He also was clearly earning the respect of his colleagues. In late June, two days after the vote for recommittal of the Court bill, Senator Edwin C. Johnson, fellow Democrat from Colorado, wrote him that although he did not agree fully with Green's stand he admired his courage and straight-from-the-shoulder approach.[10]

Rhode Island's junior senator had many other opportunities to display his loyalty to the president as open hostility to FDR increased. Roosevelt's overwhelming re-election victory in 1936, which had made him seem invincible, explains the avid way in which opponents of the New Deal seized on the inept Court reform strategy in 1937. Once the fight was over in June and the battle lost (though it was being won by changes in the Court personnel), the anti-Roosevelt forces pressed their advantage. In a few short months FDR's appearance of invincibility had vanished. Green thus became presidential champion at a time when White House stock was declining, when the domestic accomplishments of the New Deal were virtually over, and when European problems were soon to pre-empt the stage. As presidential supporter, the Rhode Islander found himself engaged in a kind of rear-guard holding operation against opponents who had tasted blood.

Hard on the heels of the Court reform defeat came the president's nomination of Senator Hugo Black of Alabama to fill the vacancy created by Justice Van Devanter's resignation. Black was a thorough-going liberal who had taken stands to the left of the administration's position on some domestic questions. Ironically, however, opponents of his confirmation uncovered the fact that Black had once belonged to the Ku Klux Klan, a revelation that seriously threatened confirmation. Black went on the radio to defend himself, acknowledging his past ties but insisting that he had long since severed his connections with the group.

Such disavowals did not satisfy Green's heavily Catholic constituency, for during the 1920s the Klan had been, if anything, more anti-Catholic than anti-Negro, particularly in the North. Nonetheless, when the question of Black's confirmation came to a successful Senate vote in August 1937, Green supported him and the president, braving the repercussions from back home. Irish constituents, for instance, denounced Roosevelt for making the nomination and suggested darkly that the senator would rue the day he voted for confirmation.[11] The protests died down, however, soon after Green's second act of vigorous presidential support.

In 1937 the president and his backers found themselves confronting the newly invigorated opposition over the issue of executive reorganization. An inevitable by-product of the rash of New Deal programs was a spate of agencies formed to carry out the new policies. Their advent on the administrative scene, plus the over-all authority claimed for the federal government over the increasingly national scope of social and economic policy, wrought massive changes in the role of the president as chief executive and chief administrator. Roosevelt's problems of supervision and co-ordination were double or treble those that had faced any predecessor.

To deal with these problems FDR appointed the Committee on Administrative Management. Two of the members, Charles E. Merriam and Luther Gulick, were political scientists; the third, Louis Brownlow, was a former journalist and District of Columbia commissioner. In their report these men began their discussion of presidential staffing with the truism "The president needs help." After recommending a battery of White House and staff aides to assist the president as chief administrator, they made sweeping suggestions aimed at streamlining the executive branch and reorganizing it into more controllable units.

When legislation to give the president the executive reorganizational powers recommended by the committee was sent to Congress, it arrived at about the same time as the Court plan. It was received, as one student of the period put it, "with sullen silence"[12] by legislators who had experienced forceful presidential leadership during the past four years and who had just witnessed the November electoral sweep. The patriarchs of the Senate balked at this new request for expanded executive authority, and many Democrats rallied behind the leadership of Harry Byrd of Virginia. But in the end, the Court fight so overshadowed other issues during the session that executive reorganization received scant attention.

Growing hostility to the president in the Congress was matched by a rising tide of hostility in the nation as a whole. To combat the New Deal with counterpropaganda, Frank Gannett and other Roosevelt opponents formed the National Committee to Uphold the Constitution. This group first played a major role in battling the Court plan, then blanketed the country with a flood of literature designed to parry what they viewed as a new attempt by Roosevelt to seize power. The committee's growing stridency and widening popular appeal prompted Roosevelt supporters to counterattack through the Senate Select Lobby Investigating Committee, which was chaired by Sherman Minton of Indiana. Green's chance to join the fray came when he replaced Hugo Black on this committee upon the senator's elevation to the Supreme Court.

In the ensuing hearings Green's defense of the administration immediately earned him the enmity of the leaders of the National Committee to Uphold the Constitution. The senators sought to discredit the committee's increasingly effective anti–New Deal propaganda by questioning the sources and uses of its ample funds. Green tried to extract an admission from Dr. Edward A. Rumely, one of the witnesses, that the committee was exerting undue pressure on key senators from important states and that it was pocketing a portion of the handsome contributions it was receiving. When Rumely denied this charge, Green sought to cast doubt on his veracity by recalling that the witness had served a prison term for pro-German activities during World War I.[13]

Despite the select committee's counterattack, the reorganization bill faced stiff resistance in 1938 when Congress reconvened. The opposition drew strength both from the ranks of the New Deal opponents, newly heartened by their success in the Court struggle, and from those in and out of Congress who saw legislative prerogative threatened by the specter of a swollen executive establishment. Nothing arouses the defensive instincts of Congress so quickly as a proposal to transfer some of its traditional authority to the rival, executive branch. When the Senate debated the bill in March, Senator Green gave it his vigorous support.

Once again his loyalty to Roosevelt provoked vigorous protests from his home state. Hundreds of letters flowed into his office, deriding his position and prophesying tyranny if the measure passed. Green, the scion of an old Yankee family, was often accused bitterly of being a traitor to his class. One correspondent demanded how Green could simultaneously support Roosevelt and be proud of his hero Roger Williams. A former governor of Rhode Island insisted that the bill was rotten and communistic. Zechariah Chafee, who had corresponded with Green on the Court plan, argued that a vote for the reorganization scheme would in effect give away some of the rights of the state and undercut the very office Senator Green held. Green replied by defending the Roosevelt proposal and by accusing the media of being biased and distorting the bill's true meaning.[14]

On 28 March a motion to recommit the bill came to a vote. Green marshaled all his arguments in a spirited defense of the president's policy, then voted against the motion, which lost, 48 to 43. He and Senator Fred H. Brown of New Hampshire were the only New Englanders who supported the president. The bill finally passed by a narrow margin. In replying to one constituent who sought to dissuade him from supporting Roosevelt, Green summed up the basis of his self-chosen role as president's man in the Senate: "It was a tremendous satisfaction when I found in President Roosevelt a leader whose views coincided with my own. I am supporting him wholeheartedly because I believe in the same objectives in which he believes, and shall support such measures as I think may attain those objectives, which I believe to be for the welfare of our country."[15]

As if to underscore this pledge of loyalty the Senator returned to Rhode Island in mid-summer 1937, at the conclusion of his first session in Congress, to give a major speech that summarized the important New Deal legislation that he had helped to enact. He pointed to the Wagner housing bill, to legislation closing tax loopholes through which many big businessmen—favorite targets of his—had been escaping taxation, and to the extension of the Guffey Coal Act, the Civilian Conservation Corps, and unemployment relief provisions. Green also expressed alarm at legislation that had failed to pass because of rising opposition to the New Deal—including bills regulating hours and setting minimum wages (later to become the last and hardest won of the major New Deal reforms), reorganizing the executive branch, and reforming the Court. In analyzing the resistance to measures in his view so urgently needed, he noted that Democrats as well as Republicans were hostile. He dismissed southern Democrats as reflecting "little more than a collection of sectional discontents and unrelated local traditions, without any basis for national existence" and accused Democrats who had been elected on the same platform as the president but had withheld their support of the administration's program of neglecting their plain duty to the president and to the voters who had elected them to further New Deal reforms.[16]

Coming from a first-session freshman senator, these were strong words; but an even stronger original draft had been toned down on the advice of Secretary of the Senate Halsey, who had warned that Democratic National Chairman James A. Farley might take exception to Green's assertion that the first session of the Seventy-fifth Congress had lacked "quality." In a striking tribute to a senator of seven or eight months' standing, the speech, with the offending words eliminated, was printed and widely distributed at the expense of the Democratic National Committee.

During the Christmas season of 1937 Green took part in a nationally broadcast round-table discussion in which he again expatiated on the philosophy of the New Deal. Capitalism must be reformed to reduce its profits and assure greater returns to laborers, it must assume responsibility for the "waste of our human resources in unemployment," and the federal government must take up the slack when private employment could not provide sufficient jobs; a primary goal of the New Deal, he argued, was to make the rules fairer "so as to give the ordinary consuming citizen a better chance."[17] Early in 1938 he presented the same views to the National Conference on Work and Security.[18] In May, in another national radio broadcast, he defended government spending for public works to stimulate the economy and advocated government limitation of work hours, an obvious reference to the Roosevelt measure pending in Congress.[19]

As supporter of the president, Theodore Francis Green took his role seriously and defined it comprehensively. He voted faithfully for the president's measures, defended them on the floor, and expounded their virtues to wider audiences whenever he could, however unpopular the cause and however much opposition the policy or his support of it generated at home. His position, he often insisted, was based on agreement with the goals of the New Deal and the objectives of the president. Reason and conscience were Green's guides, and unquestionably he was sincere. He was, however, a pro-Roosevelt politician as well as a philosophical New Deal liberal, and there were times when a purist might justifiably have claimed that his loyalty to the president was uncritical or based at best on rationalization. Green's support of the nomination of Roosevelt's old friend, Edward J. Flynn, as ambassador to Australia in 1943 is a case in point, especially in the light of the stand Green later took against President Eisenhower's nomination of Lewis Strauss as secretary of commerce. In the latter case Green felt no obligation to support the White House and also had obvious partisan motives in opposing the unpopular nomination.

Flynn, boss of the Bronx, had been made chairman of the Democratic National Committee when James Farley broke with the president over the third term issue in 1940. That the nominee had impressive qualifications as an enlightened and skillful politician, if not as a diplomat, would have been hard to dispute. One of the most intelligent and articulate men to come out of big-city politics, Flynn compared favorably with many of the businessmen and other political appointees that presidents of both parties have sent abroad to represent their country; but the odor of the Tammany machine hung heavily over Flynn.

Again Green heard from his more vociferous constituents. And Zechariah Chafee charged that Flynn's nomination discredited Roosevelt and underscored the contrast between the president's lofty ideals and his actual performance on appointments.[20] Unswayed either by such forthright opposition or by the lukewarm reaction of many Senate Democrats whose silence aided the nomination's opponents, Green supported the White House and Flynn.[21] His support was important, because Senate consideration of confirmation began with the Foreign Relations Committee of which the Rhode Islander was a member.

To the arguments that Flynn might be guilty of corruption or other wrongdoing, Green replied that the charges had never been proved.[22] Green's position was that the president should have the right to select any person he trusted for such duties unless it could be proved that the person was dishonest or unqualified.[23] Intellectually inferior as these arguments may have been, they were persuasive to Green. He voted in committee for Flynn's confirmation, and the committee narrowly approved the nomination—despite three Democratic defections. Prospects on the floor were not favorable, however, and eventually the nomination had to be withdrawn.

In the Strauss case the same arguments advanced by Republicans in defense of the president's choice for a cabinet position did not dissuade the Rhode Island Senator from joining the successful opposition. Critics could argue that his antipathy to Strauss had as pure a political basis as had his support of Flynn a dozen years earlier. But this is, after all, not really the point. While insisting in speeches and letters that his unswerving support of Roosevelt and, later, Truman was fundamentally intellectual and philosophical, Green certainly would not have denied that he was a loyal Democrat and a politician. An intellectually respectable case can be made that loyalty to one's president and party, even unquestioning loyalty, is justifiable in the name of responsible party government. It is probable that Green, like many politicians, would not have been able to sort out the partisan from the philosophical in his political motivation. He was sure, however, that support of a Democrat in the White House should be first among his senatorial priorities. In acting accordingly, he distinguished himself from many, if not most, of his colleagues.

2. New Dealer

I N the nearly four decades that have passed since 1933 there have been numerous efforts to describe the New Deal and its philosophical content. If the New Deal may be considered to have two phases, clearly Theodore Francis Green was active in Rhode Island during the early phase and arrived in Washington after the most productive period of the second. By the time he was elected to the Senate, the National Recovery Administration had been conceived, had run its haphazard course, and had been killed by the Supreme Court. Also in the past was the landmark 1935 session of Congress, in which the Social Security Act, the Wagner Act, and other measures central to the second New Deal had been enacted. Thus, Green's relation to the active period of New Deal welfare and reform legislation was indirect, through his role as governor of Rhode Island.

There is, however, a more inclusive way of characterizing the New Deal. If the term *New Deal* is used to identify an era coinciding not only with the reforms of Roosevelt's tenure as president but also with the spirit of optimistic experimentation and policy innovation of that period, it takes on a fuller meaning. Roosevelt brought to the national scene imagination and a determination to use national power to bring about change. If one uses the label *New Deal* in this sense, it applies to advances far beyond the scope of welfare and similar domestic legislation. Equally innovative were the administration's promotion of free trade after a century of tariff protection and the long campaign FDR waged to draw the United States from isolationism into an awareness of the nation's stake in the rest of the world. The protracted effort to secure approval of the St. Lawrence seaway development (unrealized until long after Roosevelt's death) also illustrates the imaginative policy proposal typical of the period. Senator Green was a New Dealer in this more comprehensive sense as well as in the consistent support he gave Roosevelt's welfare and reform legislation. The Rhode Islander, although considerably older, nevertheless shared FDR's activist approach to public policy and accepted as his own many of the goals sought by the White House.

It is paradoxical that Green, who reached maturity in the decade before the turn of the twentieth century, should have been so enthusiastic a "welfare-state liberal." In spite of his heritage from such progressive, even radical, intellectual forebears as Thomas Wilson Dorr, it is surprising that he should have embraced so enthusiastically the positive instrumental theory of government. Clearly this was no opportunistic electoral pose, for his views as governor and before are consistent with those he held in the Senate. He was convinced, as few of his generation were, of the efficacy of social legislation as a remedy for the ills and inequities of American life.

Though social security was well established when Green first arrived in Washington, he not only accepted its principles wholeheartedly but made efforts to broaden its scope. In 1941, as a member of the Senate Special Committee to Investigate Old Age Pensions, he recommended federal grants-in-aid to states for general public assistance as well as other improvements in the legislation. Taking his stand in a minority report, Green found his thinking at this point more advanced than that of his party. In 1942 he sponsored legislation to increase the amount of federal aid in the reimbursement system of federal grants-in-aid.[1] The next year, in spite of general preoccupation with the war effort, Green incorporated his ideas as expressed in the 1941 minority report into a bill introduced at the start of the session in January.[2] A few days later he defended his position in a national radio speech in which he stressed his desire to help the destitute and the medically deprived.[3]

Not merely a catchall bill introduced for effect, this 1943 legislation, designed for political feasibility, had been carefully drafted to correct deficiencies that Green perceived in existing laws. For example, he wanted to extend to both employers and the self-employed, on a voluntary basis, the coverage enjoyed by those originally included in the system. He further proposed that the benefits available on retirement also be made available not only to the worker but to his dependents as well in the case of permanent total disability. Few members of the Senate in the early forties were willing to move that fast or that far in broadening social security coverage.

Ultimate proof of Senator Green's liberal position regarding welfare is his championship of medical and hospital care legislation. Along with Rhode Island Congressman Aime J. Forand, Green took an active interest in government sponsorship of medical care, and proposals that would later be called socialized medicine were included in his 1943 social security bill. His plan called for a national health insurance program that would provide up to thirty days of fully paid hospitalization a year for an insured worker or any member of his family. Medical care for elderly persons not covered by social security would also be provided by the federal government in Green's proposal. Though proposing no change in the basic grant-in-aid matching system for financing public assistance, Green's 1943 bill also recognized that the existing formula posed serious problems. Since the system was beneficial only to the wealthier states, providing the most aid to states having the least need for federal help, he proposed increasing the amount of money given to all states whose per capita income was below the nation's average. In addition, he urged that the same principle be applied to the making of federal grants for the care of needy children.

Reaction to his bill was reasonably good in Rhode Island, but it never emerged from committee in the Senate. Not until twenty years after his 1943 proposals and four years after he had left the Senate in 1960 at the age of ninety-three did the passage of the Medicare program assure the kind of medical care that he had advocated. Green even anticipated by several years the substantial, though abortive, effort made by President Truman to secure consideration of national health insurance.[4]

The Rhode Islander's devotion to the welfare policies of the New Deal was easily transferred to Harry Truman and the Fair Deal. In 1945 he again offered legislation to extend social security.[5] At that time Democratic Senators Robert F. Wagner of New York and James E. Murray of Montana, together with Democratic Representative John Dingle of Michigan, were urging passage of their comprehensive social security program, which included a national health insurance plan. Green, however, felt that his package was politically more feasible. It included federal matching grants to states for nursing care, matching funds for general welfare grants with proportionately more made available to poorer states, lengthened periods of eligibility for both unemployment compensation and temporary disability compensation, and a 1 percent payroll tax for hospital care, either directly or through private organizations like Blue Cross. In addition to these medical care proposals in his own bill, Green strongly supported the Hill-Burton bill for hospital construction. He also urged broadened social security coverage for all gainfully employed people, including farmers. If it had been adopted, Green's proposal would have added twenty million persons to the social security rolls.

This plan, like earlier efforts, made little headway. In 1950, however, the senator had the satisfaction of seeing the enactment of legislation that gave an additional ten million people social security coverage by providing for aid to dependent and crippled children, mothers, and the permanently disabled. At length some of the reform of the welfare legislation that he had been backing became law. During the 1950s, Green continued to support any legislative proposal to improve the coverage and benefits of the social security system. Along with other liberal northeastern senators he advocated a lowered retirement age, increased benefits, more generous unemployment compensation provisions, and other liberalizing measures.

Although social welfare schemes were at the heart of the New Deal, housing and education policies were also major ingredients in the welfare state recommended by Green and other liberals. While he would have preferred stronger legislation, in 1948 he backed the Taft-Ellender-Wagner housing bill, which he insisted on calling the Wagner-Ellender-Taft bill. He also supported continuation of rent controls against an increasing postwar demand for the removal of such restrictions; favored grants of federal funds to school systems in so-called federally impacted areas; and even approved of salary supplements from the national treasury for public school teachers.

With the passage of the National Labor Relations Act in 1935, the key New Deal battle for legislation guaranteeing the rights of organized labor had been fought and won while Green was still governor of Rhode Island. Thus he had no chance to display active support in this area of reform until after the election of the Republican-controlled Eightieth Congress in 1946, in which there was more opposition to organized labor, resulting in the Taft-Hartley bill to revise substantially the Wagner Act of a dozen years before.

Senator Green made his opposition clear in a Senate speech on 7 May 1947. He praised the new era in labor relations ushered in by the earlier legislation, observing that the union movement had been freed from the shackles imposed by big business and management, and that the social as well as the economic position of the organized worker had been improved. The legislation proposed by Senator Taft and Representative Hartley, however, he termed an unfair restraint on labor activity, a punitive bill that would "necessarily weaken and embitter large numbers of organized wage earners," and "a harsh measure cleverly and carefully designed to kill labor organizations."[6] Then, with his millworker constituents obviously in mind, he recalled the long hard fight by New England labor to organize in spite of management resistance and efforts to maintain low wages and long hours. The "compact and determined opposition to unionism on the part of textile employers" in his part of the country had been vicious and unfair, Green said, and if the principles in the proposed new legislation were adopted, the progress achieved under Roosevelt and the New Deal would be in danger of destruction.[7]

This stand of the Rhode Island senator, even more than his support of New Deal social and welfare policies, aroused vociferous opposition from textile interests at home. Rhode Island textile manufacturers, like businessmen elsewhere, were convinced that labor had become too powerful, and they fervently supported the Taft-Hartley bill. Green, though keenly aware of the problems of the industry, had nonetheless long enjoyed the support of the state's growing labor movement, and he continued to assail the bill as antilabor and repressive, insisting that its real sponsor was the National Association of Manufacturers.

When the Taft-Hartley bill came to a vote, Green was one of only twenty-four senators recorded in opposition, as twenty-one of his fellow Democrats joined forty-seven Republicans to pass it overwhelmingly. Later, in the vote on the conference committee compromise version, the small band of opponents was reduced even further to seventeen, including Green and fourteen other Democrats. The Rhode Islander hailed President Truman's subsequent veto message and voted to sustain the president. Three weeks later Green joined fourteen other labor supporters in cosponsoring a bill to repeal the Taft-Hartley Act, a gallant stand that proved futile, for the bill was referred to the Senate Committee on Labor and Public Welfare, chaired by Senator Taft, where it died. Green joined in another effort to secure repeal in 1949 and took pains at every opportunity to deride the law before labor groups.

According to a CIO study of congressional voting records in

1947 Green's support of the prolabor position had been unbroken.[8] Not until 1959, near the end of his Senate career, did Green appear to waver in his steadfast sympathy to organized labor by giving lukewarm support to the Landrum-Griffin bill. By then labor was no longer the struggling, idealistic movement it had been twenty-five years before, and Green hoped that the bill would help to rid labor and management of the corruption that had crept into the ranks of both.

Besides the domestic policy reorientations it most obviously entailed, the New Deal era also saw the development of a major shift in the foreign policy emphasis of the United States. Post-World War I isolationism had found a sympathetic response in the Republican administrations of the 1920s, and even during the first year or two of the Roosevelt administration economic isolationism persisted—in the position taken at the London Economic Conference in 1933, for instance. Basically, however, FDR was an internationalist, and he had been a vigorous supporter of the League of Nations before coming to the White House; the long-term thrust of his foreign policy was clearly anti-isolationist. Sharing these impulses, Green supported the president's efforts.

The first vote cast by Green after taking his Senate seat in January 1937 aligned him with the unanimous position of his colleagues in support of an embargo on arms for either side in the Spanish Civil War. Green's involvement with the so-called neutrality legislation, as with other policy trends of the Roosevelt years, came after the initial decisions had been made, for the Neutrality Act of 1935 had already been passed to keep the United States out of future wars by embargoing American arms sales to belligerents and prohibiting the shipment of arms in American vessels to nations at war. The president, when he signed it, had commented that it was in accord with his administration's commitment "to the maintenance of peace and the avoidance of entanglements which would lead us into conflict."[9] Another act passed in February 1936 strengthened this neutrality policy and reduced somewhat the discretion left to the president.

This pattern of legislation overlooked the possibility that in some situations equal treatment of belligerents could have serious undesirable consequences. On the outbreak of the Spanish Civil War, for example, it was found that the neutrality laws applied only to national combatants, not to participants in civil strife. The embargo on arms for both sides was therefore rushed through Congress to make such coverage explicit. As time went on, however, the wisdom of this joint resolution was vigorously questioned. The existing republican government—the loyalists— badly needed outside aid in order to continue its resistance to General Franco's forces. The latter, on the other hand, received ample arms and men from the fascist dictatorships, Italy and Germany.

Both Roosevelt at the national level and Green in relation to his Rhode Island constituents felt growing cross-pressures. Liberal groups wanted the embargo removed so that the forces of democracy, as they viewed the Loyalists, could receive sorely needed assistance. Vehement Catholic opposition to the lifting of the embargo was equally understandable. The Loyalist regime was decidedly leftist and anticlerical, Communist in the eyes of some, while Franco appeared as the pious defender of the Church. Just as Roosevelt was reluctant to offend his numerous Catholic supporters by championing arms aid to the Loyalists, Green, coming from the most heavily Catholic state in the Union, likewise faced a serious dilemma. A resolution, introduced by Senator Gerald Nye of North Dakota, to raise the embargo against the legal Spanish government made the dilemma even more acute when it was referred to the Senate Foreign Relations Committee, of which Green was a member.

Contrary to his earlier view, Rhode Island's junior senator favored the Nye resolution, in spite of the fact that his Catholic constituents demanded retention of the ban on shipments to the Loyalists. The move to lift the embargo, many insisted, was anti-Christian and Communist-inspired. Many Italian-Americans in Rhode Island protested, for although support of Mussolini's regime was not widespread, ties to the mother country were strong. In light of Italy's heavy contribution of men and matériel to Franco, the Nye resolution would have placed the United States in direct opposition to Italian policy. In response to the pleadings of Secretary of State Hull, however, the committee voted overwhelmingly to defer action on the potentially controversial issue.[10]

In Rhode Island there were of course vocal Loyalist supporters who wanted the embargo raised, and they ranged from individuals who saw the Spanish conflict as a struggle for the survival of democracy against fascism to members of groups that may have been Communist. But most Rhode Islanders were on the side of the pro-Catholic and, by implication, pro-Franco forces.[11]

Nye had timed his move to coincide with congressional consideration of the whole question of the neutrality legislation. The Neutrality Act of 1936 was due to expire, and Congress ultimately voted to replace it with a permanent statute. In the latter a significant provision was added to permit materials other than arms to be sold on a cash-and-carry basis to belligerents if American financing or shipping were not involved. Green favored this bill, while his senior Rhode Island colleague, Peter Gerry, voted in opposition, believing that such a modification would undercut the purpose of the legislation, to minimize the possibility of the United States being drawn into foreign wars.

From 1937 to the attack on Pearl Harbor, Green's position essentially paralleled that of the president. Though FDR's 1937 Quarantine Speech evoked a decidedly mixed reaction that caused him to reconsider his foreign policy position, he was basically moving toward a clear antiaggressor stance. The Japanese assault on China, the German annexation of Austria, and the partition of Czechoslovakia followed in rapid succession. By 1939 FDR had embarked on a policy of strengthening the nation's defenses while still insisting that he wanted no American involvement in a foreign war. Green joined many other members of the Senate in supporting rearmament in the face of the threat posed by the dictators.

Isolationist groups in Rhode Island maintained their pressure, among them the Society of Mayflower Descendants. Green replied to the society's letters of protest that, "each one in my opinion should make his own record. If, however, distinguished descent is a basis for appeal to others, it may interest you to know that I myself am descended from a number of Mayflower *immigrants* . . . I try to do my patriotic duty as they did. I am glad to hear arguments as to why I should or should not take any particular course of action, but I have to be controlled in the decision by my own judgment and conscience."[12]

Demands from Catholic groups that the senator stand firm for American neutrality were just as likely to nettle him. One constituent warned that every Catholic in Providence was watching him and that he would lose all Catholic support in the state if he voted for lifting the embargo on arms to Loyalist Spain. To this he replied that he was sure that not all Catholics in Rhode Island supported the embargo and, furthermore, that it was "most un-American to decide questions of foreign policy on any other ground than whether it will help or hurt our country."[13]

In 1939 there was another round of debate and congressional action on the subject of neutrality legislation. A variety of proposals had been made in the Senate to change the existing provisions, some to liberalize them and some to further tighten restrictions on sales abroad for military purposes. The Foreign Relations Committee held hearings on American foreign policy during April and May. Trying to convince his colleagues that the Neutrality Act of 1937 had outlived its usefulness and was basically partial in practice, Green argued that it helped the dictators, who were not seeking our arms, and hurt countries like Britain and France, who were attempting to rearm. After considering the intricate problems involved, the committee voted by a majority of one to put off the question of revising the Neutrality Act until the next year. Green voted with the minority and issued a strong statement deploring the postponement.[14]

On 3 September 1939 war broke out in Europe. The president called Congress into special session on 21 September to urge repeal of the arms embargo, telling the legislators that he regretted signing the Neutrality Act of 1937 and that the United States had a better chance of remaining at peace through its repeal than by its continuance. Nearly two weeks earlier, in Rhode Island, Green had inferentially supported the president's as yet unannounced position by insisting in a speech that America must help the democracies against the totalitarian powers.[15]

The Senate agreed to the president's request in late October, voting 63 to 30 for repeal. In a radio speech at the time of the Senate vote, Green took a more aggressive position than the president, calling for the strengthening of our armed forces so that we could fight if the occasion demanded it. We must not become "fair game for any aggressor," he said.[16]

With the fall of France in June 1940 the popular attitude in the United States changed radically in favor of aid to Britain and of strengthening national defense. A petition from the Emergency Committee of Rhode Island with nearly ten thousand signatures urged Green to do everything in his power to provide that aid. In August he was instrumental in the passage of legislation designed to make possible the evacuation to the United States of thousands of British children. He also strongly defended President Roosevelt's agreement with Great Britain to exchange fifty overage destroyers for leased base sites in the Western Hemisphere.[17]

From then on the nation moved closer and closer to overt military aid for the beleaguered British, whose most pressing problem was the menace to their lifeline in the North Atlantic, where destroyers were desperately needed for convoy duty. Although the neutrality legislation forbade the arming of American cargo ships, in July 1941 the president ordered the navy to protect both American and Icelandic vessels sailing between the American east coast and that neutral nation. Two months later British ships were allowed to join these convoys, and, after a brush with a German submarine, orders were issued to American naval vessels on the route to shoot on sight.

An equally urgent but more intricate problem was that of making American arms and supplies available to the British. The cash-and-carry provisions in the neutrality legislation were rapidly being rendered unworkable by the imminent exhaustion of British overseas assets. In January 1941 Congress took up consideration of Roosevelt's ingenious lend-lease proposal, which did not aim at explicitly repealing the neutrality legislation but which, as isolationists in Congress made clear in voicing their opposition, did circumvent the earlier policy. In spite of isolationist opposition, however, the bill passed the House in early February and was taken up in the Senate.

Not surprisingly, Senator Green was among its most vocal proponents. In late February he spelled out the reasons for his support in a radio talk that he entitled "Aid to America." Assisting Britain, he said, was "the path of intelligent self-interest," for if Britain fell, we would be next on Germany's list; the lend-lease program would make us "in deed as well as in word, an 'arsenal of democracy.'" To those who feared that the powers the president would wield under the scheme would lead to dictatorship, Green retorted that Roosevelt's third-term victory had settled the question of whether the people trusted the president or not: "Partisanship for the sake of partisanship is a luxury which today the nation cannot afford." He then praised Wendell Willkie for supporting the measure.[18] The Senate passed the bill, 60 to 31, on 8 March 1941—amended to expire on 30 June 1943, a concession wrung from its supporters.

In October the president asked Congress to repeal the section of the Neutrality Act prohibiting the arming of ships. The House acquiesced after heated debate. Green and two other Roosevelt stalwarts in the Senate, Joshua Lee of Oklahoma and Claude Pepper of Florida, proposed repeal, as well, of the section that banned American ships from combat zones or belligerent ports. Secretary of State Hull made it clear in Foreign Relations Committee hearings that he and the president preferred a one-step-at-a-time strategy, although it was obvious that they actually supported the Green-Lee-Pepper proposal. Green's insistence on his own approach in these hearings proved embarrassing to the administration witnesses, and the president no doubt wished for somewhat less ardent assistance from his faithful supporter.[19] In effect, Green argued eloquently for the position FDR preferred but against the one the president believed politically expedient.

The Rhode Islander won his point, however, when the committee voted to report out his substitute for the House's limited repealer. The isolationists under Senator Vandenberg of Michigan fought it bitterly, urging a policy of attending solely to our own hemispherical defense. Robert A. Taft of Ohio, elected to the Senate in 1938, joined the fray on the side of his Republican colleague from Michigan. The president, now that the battle was joined, called for passage of the Green proposal in a Navy Day speech: "Our American merchant ships must be free to carry our American goods into the harbors of our friends," he asserted.[20]

Green, to support his proposal, argued that the neutrality laws were ineffectual acts of appeasement to Hitler that hindered America's efforts to help its friends and led to attacks on American ships on the high seas. Even if isolationists were not concerned about Europe, Hitler was interested in the Western Hemisphere, and it was not enough for the United States merely to manufacture war materials. This country also had to see to it that the materials reached their destination.[21]

The opponents of the measure fought to the last, but on 7 November 1941, just a month before Pearl Harbor, the Senate voted to repeal the three sections whose removal Green had been demanding for so long. His Rhode Island colleague, Peter Gerry, joined him in support of repeal. The House agreed to the Senate's broadened version, although by a narrow margin, and the president signed the bill into law on 17 November.

Senator Green was not the only member of Congress or the administration who challenged the president's judgment on the pace at which this country should proceed toward full support of Britain. In the long run Green's successful challenge probably made little difference, since the Japanese attack would undoubtedly have brought about the same result a month later. However, the episode does suggest that the Rhode Islander's support of the president could be active and imaginative. Indeed, he sometimes insisted on more vigorous means for achieving the goals he shared with Democratic White House occupants than they themselves advocated.

If Green provided continuing support for the president during the difficult years before Pearl Harbor, he was no less loyal in sustaining the administration during the war. The nation's single-minded devotion to the cause of victory did not, unfortunately, assure unanimity on methods and on the allocation of resources. In late 1942, when the United States had been officially at war for a little more than a year, the president and his advisors concluded that eleven million men were required in the armed forces to defeat the Axis powers. Such a target would obviously force total mobilization, shrink further the sector of the economy still available to fulfill civilian needs, and drain manpower from agriculture as well as vital industries.

Early in 1943 rival Senate committee investigations were launched into the question of civilian and military manpower needs, the impact of the war on the economy, and related questions. One was conducted by the Senate Military Affairs Committee under Senator Robert F. Reynolds of North Carolina, who favored Roosevelt's plans for the armed forces. In order to air his opposition to the administration manpower projections, Senator John H. Bankhead of Alabama embarked on a second investigation as chairman of the Manpower Subcommittee of the Senate Appropriations Committee. Green was among its members; one of the other four Democrats and all the Republicans on the subcommittee shared Bankhead's views.

Testimony before the Bankhead group by former President Herbert Hoover provoked Green into active defense of the administration. Hoover, whose reputation had been badly tarnished by alleged mishandling of the financial crisis that had occurred while he was in office, had begun to recover some of his high standing with the public. Moreover, since his predepression reputation was largely based on his achievements during World War I, his views carried weight in 1943. The burden of his testimony was that the figure of eleven million was too high, that so large a force would only create a shipping bottleneck, that agriculture, mining, and oil exploration must have a sufficient labor force left to them, and that time was on the side of the Allies and victory inevitable.[22]

Various prominent Democrats took issue with the former president, among them House Majority Leader John W. McCormack and Vice President Henry A. Wallace. These defenders of the administration were joined by Senator Green, who spoke out against Hoover on a nation-wide radio broadcast on 25 February. Though normally the mildest and most courteous of men, the Rhode Island senator could make as slashing a political attack as any politician, and on this occasion Green chose to label Hoover a leader of the forces of defeatism. Insisting that Hoover's plan for a smaller army would lengthen the war and cause more, rather than less, bloodshed, Green challenged advice the former president had given in 1917 as well as his recommendations for military strength in 1943. In October 1917, Green asserted, Hoover had urged President Wilson, through a memorandum addressed to White House intimate Colonel Edward M. House, to send fewer men overseas than were eventually sent. Yet, said Green, it was well known that two million fresh American troops had made victory possible. He then drew a parallel with the World War II situation.[23]

Hoover defended himself by maintaining that Green had misrepresented his testimony before the Bankhead subcommittee and, furthermore, that Green or some other person had changed the date from February 1917 to October 1917 on the memorandum to Colonel House. Green denied this but declined to say where he had obtained the documents on the grounds that to do so would only further confuse the issue. Among his papers, however, there is a typewritten copy of the memorandum, dated October 1917.[24] Obtained from the House papers at Yale by Assistant Secretary of War for Air Robert Lovett, it had presumably been forwarded to Green by the War Department. It is thus plausible to speculate that either the president or the War Department approached Green originally for aid.

As a result of this debate, the size of the armed forces was fixed at a total of 10.8 million men, which was just slightly below the original White House goal. Eventually Green and others who believed that the nation could field a military establishment of such magnitude were proved correct. (Green had argued at one point in the controversy that a nation of over 135 million people could certainly manage to put 8 per cent of that population under arms.) In recognition of the senator's contribution to a favorable outcome of the debate, Army Chief of Staff General George Marshall commended Green for ably presenting the War Department point of view and thereby rendering "the country an outstanding service."[25]

Central to Roosevelt's political leadership was his imagination and his ability to respond to the ideas of others. Among the monuments to these qualities are the great dams in the Columbia River basin and the Tennessee Valley Authority. Though less imaginative and dynamic than Roosevelt, Green, too, could respond to the potential of an idea or program. Both men saw the possibilities of a St. Lawrence–Great Lakes waterway, and while Roosevelt's interest long predated that of the Rhode Islander, Green remained to fight the battle long after FDR's death.

In 1934 the Senate failed to ratify a treaty that had been negotiated with Canada two years earlier for the development of the seaway as a joint Canadian-American venture. The politics of the project centered on a conflict of interest: midwestern industrialists and businessmen desired direct access to ocean shipping routes, while East and Gulf Coast ports, as well as the railroads connecting them with the interior of the country, feared competition from the seaway. Rhode Island was unlikely to gain or lose very much, for Providence had long since become a minor port with little to forfeit to Cleveland or Chicago, and the state was not a rail center.

The issue arose again in March 1941, when Roosevelt submitted a St. Lawrence waterway project to Congress as a defense measure. Congressional delegations from the three northern New England states bordering on Canada were divided on the alleged benefits. Senator Gerry of Rhode Island opposed the measure, but Green was neutral. When the House took no action on the measure and it failed to reach the Senate, the president tried to act through an executive agreement that would involve less congressional action. But this, too, bogged down, and no further action was taken until 1944, when Senator George Aiken, a Vermont Republican who was convinced that his state would benefit if the scheme could ever be brought to fruition, sought unsuccessfully to attach it as an amendment to a rivers and harbors bill. Green opposed the amendment because he felt so important a matter should be given full Senate consideration.

After Roosevelt died, the issue finally came up for full consideration in the upper chamber. In 1946 a resolution that favored the project and that had Green's support was reported out of the

Senate Foreign Relations Committee, but no action was taken before the election in which the Republicans won control of the Eightieth Congress. Senator Vandenberg of Michigan took over the championship of the seaway, and the Foreign Relations Committee held hearings on his bill to approve the original Roosevelt executive agreement. Representatives of midwest economic interests, former President Hoover, and Secretary of State George Marshall appeared in support of the bill; Senators Lodge and Saltonstall of Massachusetts, representatives of Louisiana, and a number of railroad executives appeared in opposition.

Reported out of committee favorably, the bill was debated on the floor of the Senate in January and February 1948. The usual regional divisions emerged, and eventually the bill was recommitted by a vote of 57 to 30. Green opposed recommitment, having finally decided to support the development of a St. Lawrence waterway. By 1951 he had become sufficiently involved in the seaway idea to introduce his own joint resolution urging ratification of the now ten-year-old executive agreement and establishing machinery for its implementation. Joined in sponsorship by twenty senators from seventeen states, Green argued that the project would facilitate transportation of iron ore and provide hydroelectric power.[26]

Over opposition from his own party he persuaded the Foreign Relations Committee to hold hearings again and worked closely with Senator Herbert Lehman of New York to line up support. In spite of resistance from fellow committee members and from Chairman Thomas Connally of Texas, Green managed to have his resolution reported out to the floor, although without committee recommendation. Taking over himself as floor manager, he joined Lehman in jousting with such opponents as Connally and Russell Long of Louisiana. Hubert Humphrey of Minnesota supported the measure, as did Republican Alexander Wiley of Wisconsin. Observing that he and the Rhode Islander often disagreed on both domestic and foreign policy, Wiley praised

Green's leadership of the bill and expressed pleasure at being on Green's side in this debate.[27]

When the roll call was finally taken, the Green measure lost 43 to 40, despite an appeal from President Truman. Once again the vote was along regional rather than party lines, with more than half the opponents from Atlantic and Gulf seaboard states. Despite this defeat Green was determined to continue the fight. The Republican victory in 1952 shifted the chairmanship of the Senate Foreign Relations Committee from the hostile Connally to the sympathetic Wiley. Wiley and Green cosponsored a bill to approve the seaway project, and Green and nine other senators simultaneously promoted a similar Democratic measure. Wiley, who saw to it that Green was made a member, himself chaired the subcommittee that considered the two measures.

Success finally came in 1954, when, with President Eisenhower's backing, the Republican House passed the necessary enabling legislation. Senate approval came on 20 January. The same pattern of opposition emerged that had always existed, with curious divisions in New England: Aiken of Vermont was for the project, while his colleague Ralph Flanders, also a Republican, was against it; and Senator John Kennedy of Massachusetts, who had replaced Lodge, voted in favor, but Saltonstall, the senior senator from the Bay State, once again registered his opposition. Both Green and his junior colleague from Rhode Island, John O. Pastore, were recorded in approval. Although Green will not go down in history as the father of the seaway idea, his role in its long gestation and final birth was by no means inconsiderable. Once he had caught the vision, he doggedly followed its implementation through to final approval.

In most of the policy decisions discussed in this chapter the senator from Rhode Island played the statesman, considering the issues on their merits, weighing them in the light of his own predispositions, and assigning his support accordingly. Although his

constituents attempted to influence his judgment at every opportunity, the cross-pressures were never severe enough to make the
choices really agonizing. Certainly Rhode Islanders, except for a
tiny minority, fully supported the welfare measures of the New
Deal. Although labor legislation may have been somewhat more
controversial, there was little question how Green's vote would
ultimately be cast, and this is true as well for foreign policy questions of the 1930s and 1940s. While the seaway project must have
been a matter of almost total indifference to the average Rhode
Islander, tariffs and reciprocal trade were different matters, for
they raised thorny issues in respect to the ailing textile industry.
A congressman is often forced to defend a local or regional economic interest at the expense of his party's platform, his president's programs or national policy, and even his own conscience.
Textiles placed Green in such a position, and the problems of
the industry were chronic concerns for him.

Because Rhode Island industry was overwhelmingly dominated by textile manufacturing, the success of southern states in
luring away many of the mills had a serious impact on the economy of the state. Green was therefore quick to act when, early in
1939, Rhode Island textile operators informed him that Golding
Brothers of New York had applied to the Reconstruction Finance Corporation for a loan of $1.6 million to finance the trans-
fer of a cloth finishing plant from Massachusetts to South Carolina. With the support of other New England members of
Congress, Green intervened with the RFC to prevent such a subsidy. Suspecting that this might not be an isolated case, the senator then introduced a bill to amend the Reconstruction Finance
Corporation Act to prohibit the making of loans for the purposes
of relocating industries.[28]

Appearing before the Senate Banking and Currency Committee, Green insisted, as the main point of his testimony, that loans
of the type he sought to proscribe were contrary to one aim of the
New Deal, that is, to distribute the national wealth more equita-

bly. If the government assisted in moving plants from regions where high wages and enlightened labor laws prevailed to poorer sections of the country, labor exploitation would continue, and the offending companies would prosper at the workers' expense. Federal money, he contended, should not be used to increase or perpetuate economic disparities between sections of the country.[29] The *Providence Journal,* though agreeing with Green's objectives, criticized the New Deal grounds chosen for his argument; its editors would have preferred a general attack on federal meddling with private business.[30] In any event, RFC Chairman Jesse Jones publicly opposed the bill, which died in committee.

In the fall of 1939 Green's concern shifted to the reciprocal trade program and its impact on textiles. The legislation granting authority to the State Department to negotiate such agreements was due for renewal. Originally, the system of reciprocal trade agreements was planned by Roosevelt and Secretary Hull as a means of lowering tariffs and gradually approaching a free trade policy for America's international commerce. The textile industry, opposing this policy and the antiprotectionist philosophy underlying it, wished instead to return to strong tariff protection against the rising tide of foreign competition for its products.

The industry was fortunate in finding for its spokesman the newly elected Republican governor of Rhode Island, William H. Vanderbilt. His was a voice that would command attention in Washington; indeed, Green and his administrative assistant Edward Higgins, alert to the possibility of Vanderbilt's building a sufficient reputation as governor to challenge Green's re-election in 1942, gave any cause that Vanderbilt espoused their careful attention.

Vanderbilt presented the case against the trade agreements and urged Green to take a stand against the program. The governor argued that many of the misfortunes that had befallen the textile industry in Rhode Island had been caused by the Roosevelt administration's free trade policies. Green replied that the reciprocal trade policy had benefited both Rhode Island and the nation as a whole; that some agreements were actually favorable to the state's jewelry, machinery, and thread industries; and that among the indirect benefits of the policy were expanded foreign markets for other Rhode Island goods. The senator urged the governor "not [to] join with isolationists in cutting down the export trade of this country as it was disastrously cut down prior to 1932" and, believing that the tariff policies of the 1920s had been partially responsible for the depression, asked Vanderbilt "to join with progressives to enlarge the markets for the products of our factories and farms . . . to provide work and increased wages for our workers and to promote the general welfare of all the people of the United States."[31]

Meanwhile, Green, who had received copies of Vanderbilt's correspondence with an assistant secretary of state assumed by the governor to be sympathetic to his views, was furnished with all the basic arguments subsequently used to refute the governor's objections to the reciprocal trade policy.[32] Vanderbilt's claims were also damaged by a marked improvement in Rhode Island Department of Labor employment figures for 1939, and even the representative of the textile industry who had been preparing its case admitted the weakness of his clients' stand.[33] In short, Green found himself in a strong position to resist powerful pressures from home and to continue his support of the trade liberalization policies of the Roosevelt administration. He relied on the president's promise that Rhode Island would not be hurt by the reciprocal trade program.

In the prewar period, then, Green staunchly supported the president's efforts to eliminate high tariffs, believing this policy to be in the interest of the whole nation; indeed, he credited the trade agreements with helping to avert isolationism. Although Green, as a New Dealer, braved pressures from constituents against the free trade policy in which he firmly believed, in the postwar period, as the problems of the textile industry became increasingly complex, he began to think along more local and regional lines. A genuine liberal in the New Deal tradition, Green stuck by his convictions, even when severely pressed from home, as long as Roosevelt, to whom he was devoted, remained in the White House. Under a new president after the war, his liberal stance lacked this additional reinforcement.

In 1948 a special subcommittee of the Senate Interstate and Foreign Commerce Committee investigated the causes of the decline of the New England textile industry but produced no tangible results. Green addressed himself to the same problem in a radio address in October of that year. Urging all those concerned to organize to stop the migration of the textile mills to the South, he deplored the manufacturers' tendency to blame the high cost of New England labor. He called on all New England members of Congress to help to equalize costs, to make New England's superior labor skill competitive by raising wages in the low-cost areas rather than lowering them in New England. Cheaper power should be made available, he declared, and Congress should assure American firms priority for their machinery orders over potential foreign competitors.[34] The last suggestion is hard to reconcile with Green's earlier position on free trade.

The conflicts between the demands of the textile operators and the policy commitments of Senator Green and Democratic liberals were generally irreconcilable, and they extended well beyond trade policy involving labor questions, issues of minimum wage legislation, power costs, and other matters. Green was host at a luncheon in Washington in June 1949 for the other New England senators, the two representatives from Rhode Island, Representatives Joseph Martin and John McCormack of Massachusetts, and leading textile plant operators.[35] Little that was promising emerged from the meeting, either for solving the industry's labor-management problems or alleviating its other difficulties.

That same year the Rhode Island senator tried to use the

Marshall Plan by attempting to persuade the Economic Co-operation Administration to purchase New England textiles for use in the European foreign aid program. He urged President Truman to intervene personally on behalf of this scheme, arguing that there had to be "some give and take for the sake of our own people," who, after all, had wholeheartedly supported the Marshall Plan.[36] The president forwarded the senator's plea to the ECA, which soon concluded that Europe produced practically all its own textile products. Green once more turned to Truman, citing New England's urgent plight, then badgered both John Steelman, assistant to the president, and Paul Hoffman, ECA administrator, about his proposal for textile purchases. Furious when he was again turned down, Green informed the president that he, McCormack, and the rest of the New England delegation had no choice but to request Truman to direct the ECA to use its funds to help the region's industry. Once more, on White House instructions, Hoffman informed the senator that nothing could be done. By this time tempers on both sides had become frayed.[37]

If Green's somewhat petulant attitude seems out of character, his behavior is at least partially understandable in the light of the pressures and frustrations implicit in this particular issue. Green represented a small, relatively poor state with a declining economy, and the textile industry's plight exemplified the state's economic problems in their most intractable form. Many efforts have been made—governmental and otherwise, here, in Britain, and elsewhere—to solve the dilemma of such declining areas but never with more than minimal success. The tragedy of this for Green was that the regional pressures generated by economic decline inevitably affected the role of statesman that he wished to play on the national level.

The senator's problem was intensified by the tendency of organized labor and management to present a united front in such a situation. In 1950 Green was thus subjected to a bombardment of communications from and on behalf of Rhode Island workers. Textile employees from Bristol, Warren, and Barrington petitioned him to resist tariff reductions, while rubber workers sent him hundreds of letters urging him to fight tariff cuts on rubber footwear. Governor John O. Pastore wrote in May on behalf of the five thousand lace workers in the state who feared that further tariff concessions would hurt their locally important industry. So large a group could hardly be ignored in spite of the desirability of supporting the reciprocal trade agreement program, and although Green later supported the Eisenhower administration's request for renewed authority to negotiate trade agreements, he undoubtedly did so with less enthusiasm than before. At the same time he sought, unsuccessfully, to have legislation passed limiting the importation of Japanese textiles.

Such political dilemmas make strange bedfellows. Henry M. Wriston, president of Brown University and a staunch Republican, had long opposed Green on both national and university policies. Wriston, however, urged the senator to stand by his internationalist views.[38] Such support must have been gratifying, although hardly sufficient to offset the counter-pressure of thousands of Rhode Island workers. Green was deeply troubled. He had supported reciprocal trade since his arrival in the Senate; during his whole political career in Rhode Island he had supported low tariff policies in the belief that they were not detrimental to the state. He was no longer certain that he had been right. In 1958 he wrote that he had become "increasingly concerned in recent years over the adverse effect which concentration of imports had upon certain segments of American industry and with serious problems which certain industries in New England have occasioned as a result of the operation of the [Reciprocal Trade] Act."[39] By the end of the 1950s, when Green evinced this concern, the tide of protectionist sentiment in Congress, if not in Rhode Island, had again receded. The executive branch was playing a greater role in making tariff decisions, and during the Kennedy administration, after Green had left the Senate, the full responsibility was lodged with the executive branch.

The issue of national trade policy versus protection for local industries is a prime example of the perennial dilemma of a member of Congress—whether to let his own convictions or his constituents' interests prevail. Green attempted to follow the former course by supporting the New Deal president in whose policies he believed. But when the economic problems of Rhode Island grew acute, the implications for his constituents of national trade policy became painfully evident, and pressures to defend home interests increased. Although he yielded, making concessions that were at times irrational or even absurd in his effort to reconcile incompatibles, he never completely abandoned his principles. Logic and consistency are not always feasible in politics. Green, however, tried harder than most members of Congress to follow those precepts, and worried more than most when he failed to do so.

3. Representative

I DEALLY, a member of Congress represents and acts for the nation as a whole throughout his term of office, considering proposed legislation from a catholic viewpoint and searching for the best solution on the merits of the proposal. Practically, however, he must often act from an entirely parochial bias. To protect the vital interests of his constituency, he must safeguard the economic well-being of his state; inasmuch as key industries often determine this well-being, frequently he must fight for the financial interests of significant businesses located within the state. Failure to do so endangers those who elected him, those who support him, and, most immediately, his future as a public servant.

Because Rhode Island is a center for the manufacture of jewelry as well as silver flatware and hollow ware, Green, throughout his Senate career, led the proponents of a free market for raw silver in their direct and ongoing confrontation with the representatives of the silver-mining states. The history of silver legislation during this period is an excellent example of interest-group politics, although, ironically, the legislating and political maneuvering never produced a result entirely satisfactory to either side. The final resolution of the problem, years after Green left the Senate, came quietly when the world market price for silver reached levels satisfactory to the silver miners and unassailable by the silver users.

Through the efforts of the silver miners and their advocates in Congress, the future prosperity of the silver-mining industry seemed assured in the 1930s. Prevailing legislation permitted unlimited mining and required the government to purchase the metal at an established price of $0.7111 an ounce. As the stock grew in the storage vaults at West Point, the value of domestic silver was protected, and by 1940 there were 1.5 billion ounces, for which the United States had paid $627 million under the provisions of the Silver Purchase Act of 1934. Legally this silver could not be sold for less than $1.29 an ounce in spite of the fact that the world price stood at about $0.35 an ounce. Since only nine states produced 95 per cent of the silver mined in the United States, it is hardly surprising that attempts to alter legislation so advantageous to the industry were heartily opposed in Congress by the silver bloc, which was comprised of the delegations from Idaho, Montana, Utah, Arizona, Colorado, and Nevada, and, to a lesser extent, those from California, New Mexico, and Texas.[1]

The first assault on the Silver Purchase Act of 1934 was made on 17 January 1939 by Senator John G. Townsend, Jr., of Delaware. Provisions of the bill he introduced to repeal the 1934 act included setting aside 500 million ounces of silver for future coinage needs, selling the remainder of the surplus on the open market, prohibiting further importation of silver, and appropriating $250,000 for research by the Bureau of Standards into new industrial uses for silver. Over the vociferous objections of the silver bloc, the Townsend bill passed the Senate in May 1940, only to die in the House Ways and Means Committee.[2]

Senator Green took no active role in this early attempt to curb the silver bloc, and there were no congressional attempts to curb it in 1941. By 1942, however, Rhode Island was beginning to feel the pinch of a raw silver shortage caused by World War II, and at this point Green became an active participant in the controversy over silver. On 30 March 1942 a committee of the New England Manufacturing Jewelers' and Silversmiths' Association met with the War Production Board and Montana Democratic Senator James E. Murray, chairman of the Small Business Committee. Murray was also a member of the Special Senate Committee on Silver, a vantage point from which he could keep a close watch on events affecting his state's silver interests. The luncheon meeting was arranged by Senator Green on behalf of manufacturers from Rhode Island who hoped to persuade the War Production Board to grant relief from the ban on the use of raw materials for nonwar manufacturing. A shortage of silver already existed, and the board would not release stocks of the raw metal for nonessential use, on the grounds that silver was badly needed in the aircraft and munitions industries because of its high electrical conductivity and its tensile strength. The board agreed to modify its ban on gold- or silver-plated copper but issued an order banning its use after 15 May 1942.[3]

By mid-July 1942 the silver situation in Rhode Island had become critical, as the shortage of silver grew more and more acute, and it appeared that many jewelry workers would have to be laid off at the end of the month, when stocks of silver would run out. Not only had bullion dealers suspended further deliveries to Rhode Island manufacturers, but the War Production Board had issued an order restricting the use of foreign silver in jewelry manufacturing after 1 October 1942.

A sense of outrage was growing within the state. Keeping a billion ounces of silver stored in the vaults at West Point, said the *Providence Journal,* was "nothing less than political blackmail" on the part of the silver bloc, and the paper urged the Rhode Island congressional delegation to take action on the problem.[4] Senator Green, however, failed in his attempt to elicit help from Donald Nelson of the War Production Board, and Senator Gerry criticized the Roosevelt administration for its lack of leadership in overcoming the recalcitrance of the silver bloc.[5] Secretary of the Treasury Morgenthau shrugged off calls for help from both Rhode Island senators.[6] Six thousand employees, about a third of the industry's labor force, had been cut from the payrolls of Rhode Island firms, and by mid-July 1942 the outlook for the state's jewelry industry was indeed bleak.[7]

Even though the ban on importing foreign silver for nonessential use did not go into effect until after 1 October 1942, Rhode Island manufacturers found it virtually impossible to buy silver from Mexico prior to the deadline; but in mid-August they finally arranged to purchase half a million ounces of silver from Mexico at $0.55 to $0.65 an ounce. When the federal government used the emergency powers granted to the executive branch in time of war to forbid the use and further purchase of such silver on the grounds that the price was above the ceiling of $0.3537 an ounce, 133 Rhode Island silver manufacturers, employers of 99 per cent of the state's 25,000 jewelry workers, appealed to their congressional delegation.[8]

In mid-September 1942 the Treasury Department was buying domestic silver at the established price of $0.7111 an ounce, twice the normal price for imported silver, while holding 3.331 billion ounces. Of this amount, 806 million ounces were in the form of silver coins; 1.164 billion ounces were pledged against silver certificates; and 1.361 billion ounces were lying unused underground at West Point. Since the Treasury Department continued to purchase silver at the rate of 70 million ounces a year, the manufacturers asked to have the stored silver freed for their use.

The War Production Board took the position that restrictions could not be loosened because silverware and jewelry were luxury commodities.[9] The manufacturers next tried to obtain an executive order authorizing transfer to them of the stored silver for civilian use. The attorney general stated that such a transfer would be illegal and refused to listen to Green's arguments. The suggestion that these Rhode Island firms convert completely to war industry was unfeasible, since the conversion would have been difficult and expensive. Moreover, a number of the small plant owners claimed that the government was not giving them a fair chance to procure orders, if indeed they were being considered at all.

In his next move to help the distressed industry, Green decided to avoid a direct confrontation with the powerful silver bloc by drafting a bill that would differ radically from previous attacks on the Silver Purchase Act of 1934. His plan was to persuade Congress to authorize the executive branch to release a sizable portion of the stored silver for domestic use. In Green's bill such released silver would be employed "strictly in connection with the war effort"; this wording, he hoped, would permit the release of silver for civilian use when it was shown that the government had a sufficient supply for producing war matériel. Green proposed, furthermore, to return to the government "any silver sold or leased . . . not actually used in connection with the war effort" within one year after the termination of the war.[10]

Unlike Representative Emanuel Celler, Green made no attempt to repeal the Silver Purchase Act of 1934. While Celler wanted to remove from the statute books the "entangling skeins skillfully woven by the so-called 'silver bloc'" and force the Treasury Department to "lift its hands off this buried silver" altogether, Green only wanted to pry 30 million ounces of silver from the vaults at West Point for his state's needs.[11]

Upon referral to the Senate Banking and Currency Committee, the bill gained immediate support from the New England Manufacturing Jewelers' and Silversmiths' Association and from the Silver Users' Emergency Committee, which was composed of twenty large silver-using eastern manufacturers under the chairmanship of Rhode Island jeweler William G. Thurber. Senator Patrick McCarran of Nevada, the strong man for the silver bloc, claimed that the administration did not particularly favor Green's bill, that the silver senators from the West had agreed to oppose it, and that he would soon introduce a bill in the Senate to raise the government purchase price of domestic silver from $0.7111 to $1.29 an ounce, $1.29 being the price below which the government was not permitted to sell. The executive secretary of the Prospectors and Mine Owners Association at first accused Green of impugning the integrity and motives of the silver bloc, but after reading the bill, he commented favorably on Green's fairness. Nonetheless, to the silver bloc in the Senate, Green was now anathema.[12]

Welcome aid came from Walter E. Spahr, professor of economics at New York University and secretary-treasurer of the Economists' National Committee on Monetary Policy. Spahr, an antisilver economist who viewed Green's bill as a vehicle for facilitating the adoption of inconvertible paper money, theorized that the release of the stored silver for industrial use would indirectly make the policy of issuing silver certificates pointless. Apparently concurring with Spahr's argument, Green claimed that his bill would permit the Treasury Department to lend the silver retained as a pledge against the issuance of silver certificates for nonconsumptive purposes; silver lent for such uses as making bus bars would back silver certificates just as effectively as if it remained in the vaults. Indeed, Green saw no reason why the government could not freely sell the stored silver for consumptive purposes.[13]

Donald Nelson, chairman of the War Production Board, stated that he would not object to the Green bill if it provided for board involvement in decisions concerning the release of silver for civilian use. Since control of priorities and allocation of vital matériel were essential to Nelson's function, Green agreed to insert a provision giving the board a major voice in the allocation of the silver. Also at Nelson's request, it was stipulated that the average price of the silver sold by the government to civilian industry would not be less than $0.50 an ounce.[14]

Hearings on the Green bill were held on 14 October 1942 before a subcommittee of the Senate Banking and Currency Committee. To the claim that a number of eastern manufacturers would be forced out of business because of the silver shortage, Green answered that silver was to be released for civilian use only when it would not conflict with the war effort; the manufacture of knives, forks, and spoons would never be put ahead of tanks. He further asserted that only 30 million ounces of silver would be needed to keep the civilian industry alive during

1943.[15] Two days after the hearing the subcommittee approved the bill.

The second session of the Seventy-seventh Congress was drawing to a close, and by the end of October the silver users feared that the bill would never be reviewed by the full committee because Senate interest in the matter was not high. However, at the insistence of Senator McCarran, who opposed the measure, the full Banking and Currency Committee held another hearing on 1 December. Since there was no grave opposition outside of the silver bloc, the bill was approved on 3 December. The Senate report noted that the president could release silver by either selling or leasing on the recommendation of the War Production Board and with the advice of the secretary of the treasury whenever deemed advisable for the war effort. The silver was to be used "in the making of munitions, the supplying of civilian needs in connection with the war effort, and the conversion of existing plants for such purposes, so that consumptive as well as non-consumptive uses may be taken into account."[16] The average price for all the silver sold was to be not less than $0.50 an ounce, and authorization to sell silver in this way was to end on 31 December 1944.

Determined to filibuster the bill to death, McCarran began delaying tactics even before it reached the Senate floor. He termed the proposal an attempt "to reduce the price of silver in the open markets of America, so that it may be used in the making of gewgaws, in the making of flatware, in the making of knives and forks and spoons."[17] The measure was killed in the closing days of the session. The Seventy-seventh Congress, which had declared war and then spent twelve months devising legislation to conduct it, was in no mood to consider the parochial needs of a few New England states.

On 3 January 1943 Senators Green, McCarran, and Murdock of Utah, discussed the bill on the radio program "American Forum of the Air." Green stressed the fact that he was not attacking the monetary use of silver and urged support for his new Senate bill. McCarran charged Green with representing only a selfish segment of the economy that produced nonessentials and wanted to make huge profits by paying only $0.50 an ounce for government-stored silver. Furthermore, McCarran argued, the Treasury Department had acquired silver "solely for use as money," and it was not intended for any other purpose. Murdock labeled the bill superfluous and challenged it as an outright attempt to depreciate the monetary function of silver regardless of assertions to the contrary.[18]

Several silver bills were introduced in the first few days of the Seventy-eighth Congress. While Green submitted another bill to make silver available for consumptive use, Murdock proposed legislation to ensure that such silver would be sold at $0.7111 an ounce rather than at the $0.50 an ounce price that Green requested. McCarran introduced a measure to guarantee that silver stockpiled by the government would never fall below the amount necessary to back the silver certificates issued by the Treasury Department. In the House, Representative Celler attached a rider to the annual treasury and postal appropriations bill that would have forbidden the Treasury Department to purchase additional silver from any source; if passed, the amendment would, in effect, have repealed the Silver Purchase Act of 1934. Celler's rider so infuriated the silver bloc in the Senate that McCarran and Murdock vowed to hold up the treasury and postal appropriations rather than see it approved.[19]

Meanwhile, a subcommittee of the Senate Banking and Currency Committee was considering the bills introduced by Green, McCarran, and Murdock. At hearings on 28 and 29 April 1943, Green testified that silver was not money but only a commodity and that it was needed in industry. Since importation of foreign silver had decreased and production of domestic silver was insufficient to meet the needs of the nation, he argued that legislation should be passed releasing the government stores of silver for consumptive use. Once again Green's bill called for setting the selling price at no less than $0.50 an ounce. McCarran vigorously objected to silver being called a commodity and attacked the price of $0.50 an ounce, which he insisted be raised to $0.7111 an ounce. First the subcommittee and then the full committee backed the Green bill, although it was amended to include the $0.7111 provision, to require the retention of enough silver by the government to back the issuance of silver certificates, and to terminate the authority to sell or lease the silver six months after the end of the war.[20]

On 17 May 1943, when Green asked for the unanimous consent of the Senate to consider his proposal, Murdock stated that he would oppose such consideration until the Celler amendment had been removed from the appropriations bill. McCarran, too, was still hesitant; however, when Celler agreed to withdraw his amendment, McCarran raised no further objection, apparently satisfied at last that Green's bill, as amended according to his and Murdock's requirements, did not "by word or intendment" affect, limit, or impair the laws with respect to "acquisition, retention, and price of silver."[21] On 18 June 1943 the bill unanimously passed the Senate and went to the House. Although Celler expressed the opinion that the nation was still "a bunch of suckers to the foreign silver producers," he nonetheless termed the bill the best possible one under the circumstances.[22] The House passed the bill, and President Roosevelt signed Public Law 137 with a pen given to Green by the New England Manufacturing Jewelers' and Silversmiths' Association.[23]

The bill as passed was clearly a compromise. Green wished silver to be available for industrial use, and the silver senators wanted to make sure that the mining interests would continue to be protected. More interested in the release of silver than in its price, Green was forced to go along with a price of $0.7111 an ounce to assure passage of any bill at all. By mid-November 1943,

22.855 million ounces of silver had been released from government vaults, and substantial amounts of it went into the production of engine bearings, brazing alloys, and solders; very little of it was used to produce nonessential goods.[24]

By May 1944, with the Green Silver Act due to expire on 31 December, silver once again loomed as an issue. Celler had vowed to repeal the Silver Purchase Act of 1934; he believed that the Green Silver Act had resulted in a "modicum of relief" but was convinced that the subsidies themselves had to be eliminated. Silver, Celler said, was an "obelisk . . . built to false gods."[25]

Hoping to encounter less difficulty than before because silver was less in demand for nonessential manufactures, Green introduced a bill in the Senate to extend the Silver Act for two years. Senator Maloney of Connecticut, chairman of the Senate Banking and Currency subcommittee that was studying the bill, pointed out that very little silver had actually been acquired for civilian use because most of the silver manufacturing plants had converted to war work. It was argued that the Green Silver Act should be extended to protect workers in the silver industry against government cutbacks and war contract cancellations as the war drew to a close. It was also feared that the silver bloc senators would be able to raise the price of domestic silver if the act were allowed to expire. On the other hand, the silver bloc wanted to protect fully the employment of silver as money and feared losing ground to easterners who viewed silver primarily as a commodity. Evading the major problems of subsidies to the silver mining states, a price increase for domestic mined silver, and the continued use of silver in the bimetallic monetary policy of the United States, the Senate Banking and Currency Committee extended the Green Silver Act for one more year. The bill passed both houses easily.[26]

Once again, on 20 June 1945, Green attempted to have his act extended.[27] The war in Europe had ended, however, and the silver bloc intensified its campaign to retain the monetary value of silver and to increase the price paid for the domestic mined metal. When the war in the Pacific ended, Green could no longer justify his bill as a war measure, the guise under which it had passed in 1943 and 1944. Forced to change his tactics and his general line of argument, the Rhode Island senator on 24 October introduced a bill that would have authorized the Treasury Department to sell or lease for the next two years any of its stockpiled silver not essential for the backing of silver certificates at the price of $0.7111 an ounce.[28] This proposal was the first outright attack that Green made on the position of the silver senators.

Unable to stop this move, the silver bloc was nonetheless determined to raise the price paid for newly mined silver. In October Senator McCarran introduced a bill to raise the price of silver to $1.29 an ounce. The jewelry industry in Rhode Island naturally hoped to keep down the cost of reconverting to a peacetime economy, and Green therefore opposed McCarran on the price increase. Importation of silver had practically ceased, so that the jewelry and manufacturing industry could survive only through the release of government-owned silver. McCarran and his colleagues from the West feared that a large-scale release would force the price of silver down still further.

Green garnered strong support for his view from the administration. Chester Bowles, head of the Office of Price Administration, thought that extending the Green Silver Act at a price of $0.7111 an ounce would be conducive to both reconversion and stabilization. The head of the Civilian Production Administration, J. D. Small, believed that Green's bill was highly desirable because, in his opinion, there was sufficient silver at $0.7111 an ounce to meet the demand. The Treasury Department also approved the bill.[29]

Republican Representative Joseph W. Martin, Jr., of Massachusetts, in whose state were numerous jewelry manufacturing firms, decided to represent these interests by introducing a bill that was identical to Green's. Passed by the House on 19 December 1945, Martin's bill, upon reaching the Senate, was referred to the Banking and Currency Committee that was still holding Green's bill. After the Green Silver Act expired on 31 December, the shortage of silver intensified. The Senate committee was deadlocked over the matter, and Representative Martin, taking a cue from Representative Celler, attached the Green bill as a rider to the annual treasury and postal appropriations bill. Although the silver senators were annoyed at this maneuver, the House recognized the need of the silver manufacturing industry for 100 million ounces of silver and passed the appropriations bill with its rider.[30]

At this point, the main debate on the price of silver shifted from the Senate Banking and Currency Committee to a subcommittee of the Senate Appropriations Committee. The silver bloc testified that the western states had suffered unduly because of the low price of $0.7111 an ounce paid by the Treasury Department for newly mined silver; silver miners testified that they could not operate their mines profitably and that the price should therefore be raised to $1.29 an ounce. It was argued that it was in the interest of the economy not only to have the Treasury Department retain its stock of silver but also to raise the price the Department paid for it. It was argued further that if the department holdings were thrown on the open market as Green recommended, the price would drop even lower and wipe out the silver mines altogether. Several silver bloc senators and many of the testifying mine owners attacked the integrity of the jewelry manufacturers, claiming that the easterners made exorbitant profits and could easily afford to pay $1.29 an ounce for silver.[31]

Some opponents attacked the status of the silver proposal as a rider to the appropriations bill, but Green defended it, stating, "we cannot sit in judgment on the House. It comes to us as an

appropriation bill from the House, and any question as to legislation, whether it is legislation or not, is decided in the House
and we have no right to change it."[32] Certain that the subcommittee would try to do so, Green lost his usual imperturbability
and grew noticeably annoyed as the hearings wore on.

When it became obvious that a compromise was necessary,
McCarran finally offered to accept the release clauses of the easterners' request if they would agree to a price of $0.903 an ounce
for the first year and $1.29 an ounce after 30 June 1948. Green
assumed that this might be the best compromise he could effect
and invited four of the leading Rhode Island silver users to meet
with Senators Tydings, Walsh, Bridges, Wherry, and Saltonstall,
of the Appropriations Committee. They agreed to McCarran's
offer, and the Senate then approved the compromise on 21 June
1946.[33]

However, Representatives John W. McCormack and Joseph
W. Martin, Jr., both of Massachusetts, assailed the Senate action
and led the House in declining the Senate version by a vote of
266 to 22.[34] Senator McCarran vowed to block the release of silver until the House agreed to a higher price. Although Green
attempted to persuade the Senate to accept the lower price of the
House version, the Senate struck out the amendment rider from
the appropriations bill and suggested a permanent price of
$0.903 an ounce, which it hoped the House would accept. Green
expressed satisfaction and described the Senate action as a "considerable whittling down of the demands of the silver bloc," but
the House refused to accept the compromise.[35]

On 12 July 1946 Green defended the position of the House in
a debate with Senator Kenneth McKellar of Tennessee, a close
friend of Senator McCarran. McKellar chastized the eastern jewelers for charging high prices and making outrageous profits on
silver products. If the selling price of government-owned silver
remained at $0.7111 an ounce, he argued, the jewelry industry
would make even greater profits because the open market price

had risen to $0.90 an ounce. Green moved that the Senate accept the $0.7111 an ounce price that the House suggested, but his motion was overwhelmingly defeated, 54 to 25.[36]

Senate conferees, led by Carl Hayden of Arizona and McKellar, met, Green among them, with representatives of the House. It was glaringly apparent to the House conferees that McKellar would not back down and that there would be no agreement at all unless they finally agreed to a higher price. The House therefore retreated from its position, and a compromise price of $0.905 an ounce was set. The measure was eliminated from the appropriations bill, and Representative Martin's original bill was substituted. The government was to buy all domestic mined silver at the higher price of $0.905 an ounce but would now be allowed to sell its surplus at the same price. The bill became law on 31 July 1946 and had no expiration date.[37]

Because of his vigorous efforts on their behalf over the years, Green now had the solid backing of Rhode Island's jewelry manufacturers. William F. McChesney, vice-president of the Gorham Silver Manufacturing Company, told Green that the jewelry industry owed him immense gratitude for his Senate leadership on legislation to release silver from the government vaults.[38]

On 6 January 1947 Senator McCarran, seeking to ease the financial burden of the silver miners, proposed a bill that would have permitted a federal district or state court to give mortgage moratorium relief to any individual or firm contracting, or having an option to work, a silver or gold mine but unable to exercise the option "for reasons beyond his control." Although McCarran had been introducing such legislation to protect silver mine owners since 1943, it had never been acted on. This time the Senate Judiciary Committee, of which McCarran was chairman, reported out the proposal; Green, however, objected to giving the unanimous consent necessary under Senate rules to permit consideration of the bill on the grounds that the expression "for reasons beyond his control" had far-reaching significance. He wanted to know what economic effect the bill, if enacted, would have. Much to McCarran's annoyance, the bill had to be passed over. When McCarran failed to spell out the economic implications of the bill to Green's satisfaction, the Rhode Island senator objected to unanimous consent of the Senate three more times, and the bill died.[39]

The silver bloc, however, had become less demanding as the world price of silver dropped. By June 1947 the world price hovered at about $0.60 an ounce, while domestic silver was still protected at $0.905. But Green, whose relationship with the silver industry in Rhode Island was growing even closer, was proud of his success against the silver bloc and determined to continue his opposition to McCarran. In mid-January, at the request of Green's administrative assistant, McChesney agreed to chart the course of action the industry wished the senator to follow. When the Silver Users' Committee adopted a program to promote free silver and unrestricted marketing, McChesney urged Green to continue the fight against the silver bloc. In this connection Green tried unsuccessfully to convince the State Department that a representative of the jewelry industry should be among the delegates to the Geneva Conference on Trade Negotiations.[40]

During this period, Green turned his speech writing over to retired Rear Admiral Donald J. Ramsey, the chief lobbyist and treasurer of the Silver Users' Association. An antisilver article Green wrote for the *American Magazine* was found deficient by McChesney, and Green permitted one of the silver manufacturer's men to rewrite the article. When the magazine rejected the second version, Ramsey was assigned the task of writing a new one to be submitted over Green's signature. Although the *American Magazine* once again rejected the article, the episode illustrates the close ties between Green and the industry.[41] Statistical information from the Treasury Department or the Bureau of

Mines was obtained for the silver users by Green's office; in return, Ramsey supplied the senator's office with data, speeches, and suggestions.

In late 1947 the silver users feared that the silver bloc, in an attempt to increase the demand for silver and thus create a higher price, would try to persuade the federal government to lend silver to China to support the sagging economy of the Chiang Kai-Shek regime. When McChesney urged Green to oppose such a measure, the Treasury Department assured Green that the government was not contemplating such a plan.[42]

Green was neither unaware of, nor unsympathetic to, the plight of the small mine operators in the Mountain States. While they were caught between the high production costs and relatively low prices, a few large mine operators were prospering as a result of the government purchase policy. Enforced silver buying, Green told a Providence radio audience, was "the most atrocious example of special privilege furthered by law to be found in American history." Huge subsidies were being paid to American producers of silver when the storage vaults at West Point were filled with millions of ounces of silver "for which we have no need, and for which we have paid more than the market price." Industrial users were forced to depend on foreign silver at an artificially high price because the American policy of buying up domestic mined silver created a shortage. The time had come, he said, to repeal the "infamous" Silver Purchase Act of 1934. Green assured his friends in the silver and jewelry industries of his continuing efforts on their behalf.[43]

Aware that the Treasury Department was now fully behind efforts to repeal the act, Green decided in December 1949 to introduce both a repeal bill and a bill authorizing an investigation of the alleged collusion of the miners to set the price of silver. There was some doubt that these bills would ever be reported out by the Senate Judiciary Committee because of the continued influence of the silver bloc senators. Green's administrative assistant, Higgins, had already spoken to the chief of the Antitrust Division of the Department of Justice about the possibility of investigating manipulatory practices of the silver producers, but the Justice Department had done nothing, and Higgins was sure that McCarran had managed to stop such an investigation.[44]

On 11 January 1950 Green introduced his bill for the repeal of the act.[45] Substantially written by Admiral Ramsey of the Silver Users' Association, the bill, besides repeal, called for retention of 371.25 grains of silver (in bullion or in silver dollars) for each dollar of silver certificates outstanding and for conversion of all the surplus metal to silver dollars. Senator Paul Douglas's Subcommittee on Monetary, Credit, and Fiscal Policies of the Joint Committee on the Economic Report strongly backed repeal of the Silver Purchase Act of 1934; Douglas himself stated that he could see only sixteen reasons for the purchase policy of the United States—the sixteen senators from the Mountain States. The Economists' National Committee on Monetary Policy recommended enactment of the Green bill and its companion in the House introduced by Representative Aime Forand of Rhode Island.[46] For the opposition, McCarran charged that the people behind Green were interested in destroying America's entire monetary system and that the bill was "an irresponsible attempt to ruin Western miners for the sake of cheap silver sought by a few greedy silver manufacturers on the East Coast."[47] Then, on 28 February, McCarran introduced a resolution to investigate monopolistic practices by bullion brokers and jewelry manufacturers, charging that the easterners were arbitrarily depressing the price of domestic silver. (This move seemed ironic to William F. McChesney, who believed that the bullion dealers were in league with the silver mine operators.) McCarran's bill was referred to the Senate Judiciary Committee, of which he was the chairman, and Green's bill went to the Banking and Currency

Committee. Because the time was not yet propitious for relegating silver to a nonmonetary position, Green's bill was never reported out by the committee; McCarran's bill was also held in reserve and never considered.

Over the next two years the world price of silver rose steadily. While the silver users, on the one hand, kept up a steady barrage of propaganda against the silver purchase policy of the government, the silver mine operators, on the other hand, pressed their demands for a higher subsidy. Once again, McCarran aimed at $1.29 an ounce for domestic mined silver. Postwar developments in the employment of silver in industry and the arts had virtually demonetized the metal. At the same time, silver output had dropped to 40 per cent of the immediate pre–World War II period. Government stocks at West Point increased as silver flowed back to the vaults from its nonconsumptive use in World War II. Most of it came from the Atomic Energy Commission's jurisdiction. Silver had been used extensively in the large electromagnetic plant at Oak Ridge, but conversion to another method of processing uranium had made the silver superfluous, and silver worth $400 million was returned to government stocks.[48]

On 14 March 1955, again introducing a bill to repeal the Silver Purchase Act of 1934, Green was joined in sponsorship by Senators Douglas of Illinois, Bush and Purtell of Connecticut, Kennedy and Saltonstall of Massachusetts, and Pastore of Rhode Island. Backed by the New England Senators Conference, the bill was presented on behalf of the silver users, who felt that Treasury Department purchase of domestic mined silver was holding the price of the metal artificially high. Silver had been rising steadily on the world market and had reached about $0.90 an ounce, the highest price in thirty-five years.[49]

By his own admission, Green's position on silver was dictated by his state's economic interests: he was politically motivated first and concerned only secondarily with the position of silver in the nation's monetary system. It was merely by accident that "intelli-

gent and disinterested economists" were on his side; nevertheless, Green defended his bill on monetary grounds, believing

> in the free enterprise system with a free and open market
> operating generally under the laws of supply and demand. If
> any industry suffers injury, it may come to the Congress
> with its problems and seek relief. But, no industry should be
> guaranteed either a subsidy at the expense of our monetary
> system, or a fixed price without any regard for need. Repeal
> of the silver purchase laws would both correct the existing
> unsound monetary condition, and also provide a free and
> open market for silver. The silver-using industry seeks no
> subsidy, no guaranteed price for its products. No one can
> foretell whether the price of silver in the market will go up
> or down.[50]

The silver bloc asked the chairman of the Banking and Currency Committee, Senator J. William Fulbright, to postpone the
hearings indefinitely, but Senator Douglas, as chairman of the
subcommittee, held them anyway. While the assistant secretary
of the interior defended the silver-buying program as necessary
to keep the basic metal mines in operation, economists attacked
the governmental subsidy as contributing nothing to the sound-
ness of the nation's monetary system and as having no social benefit. Since the congressional session was nearing its end, the hearings were postponed until 1956 to permit the silver bloc to
gather testimony. When the hearings were resumed, the silver
mine operators did not appear but submitted their objections in
writing.[51]

Green's proposal to repeal the Silver Purchase Act of 1934 was
killed in the 1956 session when Senator Wallace F. Bennett of
Utah, one of the three Republicans on the subcommittee, read
to the members a letter from the chairman of the House Banking and Currency Committee stating that his committee's busy
schedule would prevent it from considering two bills during that

session of Congress. Neither of these bills had any bearing on Green's proposal, but when Bennett read the letter—mistakenly, he later claimed—he referred to the bills by number rather than by title or description. Bennett then moved to table Green's bill on the ground that there was little point in further consideration if no House action was possible, and the subcommittee, unaware that the letter did not refer to the silver bill, voted for his motion.[52]

After the 1956 election Green became chairman of the Foreign Relations Committee and consequently had less time to devote to the silver interests in his state. By 1960 the industrial demand for silver had increased markedly. Since a sizeable supply of the metal was still being retained by the Treasury Department for monetary purposes, the silver users again urged what amounted to the complete demonetization of silver: the repeal of the Silver Purchase Act of 1934 and the release of all available silver for industrial use. As one of his last legislative acts the ninety-two-year-old Rhode Islander introduced a repeal measure in April 1960, but ill health had already forced him to give up the chairmanship of the Foreign Relations Committee, and he was unable to campaign for his proposal, which was never considered.

4. Legislator

EMBERS of the United States Congress actually make laws. It is customary for a representative or a senator to develop an idea, introduce a bill, and then work assiduously to promote its passage. Indeed, the fame of a member of Congress frequently rests on the major pieces of legislation that carry his name in their official designation, and in many cases his involvement results from an idealistic desire to promote the national well-being rather than from party or local pressures. Although Theodore Francis Green was not renowned for his legislative efforts, he made a noteworthy contribution to laws controlling absentee voting.

In July 1942 Senator Green and Representative Robert L. Ramsey of West Virginia, another Democrat, introduced companion bills in their respective houses to provide for absentee voting for members of the armed forces stationed within the continental limits of the United States. This relatively simple proposal—which, however, was an innovation in American politics—had germinated in the mind of Senator Green, who firmly believed that servicemen should have the privilege of voting for federal officials. The bill authorized the war and navy secretaries to provide post cards to servicemen for requesting ballots from their home states: on receipt of the post card, the secretary of state of the serviceman's home state was to send a special "federal" ballot listing the candidates for federal offices; if the laws of the state were amenable, a ballot listing candidates for state office might also be included. After marking the ballot, the serviceman was to return it to his state for inclusion in its electoral count. The bill did not provide for voting by servicemen overseas, on the grounds that such a plan would be difficult to administer and might lead to breaches of military security. Nor did it exempt servicemen from paying the poll tax in the eight southern states that required it.[1]

Democratic Representative John E. Rankin of Mississippi led southern resistance to the bill as an invasion of states' rights by the federal government. Most southerners regarded even a weak law as a step in the direction of federal regulation of state elections, a prospect they viewed with indignation, if not horror. In spite of Rankin's obstructionist tactics of demanding several quorum calls and his bitter attack on the Ramsey proposal, the House, clearly aware of the small impact the bill would have on the 1942 elections, passed the measure by a vote of 134 to 19.[2]

In the Senate, the bill was referred to the Committee on Privileges and Elections, of which Green was chairman. After brief hearings, Green, on behalf of his committee, recommended passage of the House measure and suggested its immediate consideration because election day was imminent. As floor manager for the measure, Green pointed out that Congress, under Article I, Section 4, of the Constitution, could make rules governing election to Congress, and that the major objective of the bill was to give the vote to servicemen who had been unable to register in their home states. No attempt was being made, he argued, to alter such state-devised qualifications for voting as age, residence, or poll-tax payment; moreover, the bill was intended to apply to general elections, not state primaries. The bill, he said, merely extended the election laws of the states by providing election machinery for states that had no absentee voting laws and by supplementing the laws of the states that already possessed such provisions. Thus, the soldier absentee voting law would not conflict with state law but would complement it. In states that had absentee voting legislation, the federal law would simply give the serviceman a choice between the federal ballot and the regular state absentee voters ballot.

In opposition, Senator Walter George of Georgia contended that the bill would result in undesirable federal meddling, whatever its intent. Green countered by noting that the federal government was only providing post cards and that he was not supporting a bill that would encroach upon state elections. To the suggestion, made by Senator Arthur Vandenberg of Michigan, that a state be permitted to exempt itself from the federal law if it had suitable legislation covering absentee voting, Green replied that state laws were so diverse that exemption would defeat the whole objective of easing the voting procedure for servicemen. If both a federal and a state ballot were available, a serviceman could select the one he preferred. Green further assured the Senate that safeguards existed that permitted a state to accept only the ballots of voters who were qualified under its laws, so that the states retained their right to determine the legal qualifications for voting.[3]

To speed passage of the House-approved bill, Green attempted to prevent the addition of controversial amendments to the proposal, although he agreed to a change of wording explicitly limiting the application of the absentee voting law to those who met state qualifications. Two additions were made nonetheless: the first, to ensure servicemen the vote even if they had not paid their poll taxes; the second, to extend the bill's coverage to include primary elections involving federal candidates. In spite of these explosive additions, the bill passed easily, 47 to 5.[4] As leader of the Senate conferees, Green was able to persuade the House members to accept the Senate version of the bill. Since time was very limited and the representatives did not wish to be accused of being unpatriotic, Public Law 712 went into the statute books on 16 September 1942, just in time for token use in the November elections.

This Absentee Voting Act of 1942 was cumbersome: the distributing of post cards by the Departments of War and of the Navy, the handling of requests for a federal ballot from the separate states, and the dispatching of different forms of these ballots by the states to the servicemen all made implementation exceedingly difficult. Only twenty-eight thousand of approximately five million eligible voters actually cast votes under the new system.[5] And in Congress, doubts about the law remained. The suspension of the poll tax for servicemen was particularly repugnant to the southern Democrats, wary as they were of any loosening of state or federal law that might allow Negroes to gain the franchise. Republicans, anticipating the 1944 election and certain that many servicemen would vote for their commander-in-chief, had no desire to give Roosevelt a ready-made constituency. Because the Roosevelt Democrats, also contemplating the future, wanted the law strengthened to provide a significantly larger service vote, Senators Green and Scott Lucas attempted in 1943 and 1944 to pass a more effective law. In the 1942 election barely three hundred Rhode Island servicemen had cast absentee ballots; Green wanted to increase this number, not only for his own political benefit, but also because he believed that servicemen had a right to vote.

Reliable estimates indicated that ten million servicemen and women would be old enough to vote in the 1944 presidential election. The vast majority would be too far away to cast their ballots at home and would therefore have to depend on the various state procedures for absentee voting, most of which had been devised for peacetime balloting. Although the time involved in requesting, receiving, and returning ballots precluded voting by military personnel stationed overseas or in distant parts of the United States, absentee votes—or a lack of them—could nonetheless determine the outcome of the 1944 presidential contest. No official announcement had been made, but it was generally assumed that Roosevelt would be a candidate for a fourth term. The Republicans were uncomfortably aware of the armed forces' view of Roosevelt as a magnetic, inspiring commander-in-chief; however, they could ill afford to appear to thwart a proposal designed to facilitate absentee voting for servicemen.[6]

Sparse voting by servicemen in 1942 had not threatened white domination of the political systems in the southern states. However, southerners hoped to prevent the extension of the provision of the 1942 law that temporarily absolved servicemen from poll taxes; they believed that the provision encouraged Negroes to seek voting rights.

Northern Democrats who displayed an altruistic desire to obtain the vote for servicemen fighting throughout the world also were aware that the vote of these young people would be overwhelmingly Democratic. Senators Green and Lucas, as well as Representative Eugene Worley of Texas, were motivated by both considerations when, in June 1943, they introduced identical bills in the House and the Senate to amend the Absentee Voting Act of 1942 to provide the vote for servicemen overseas as well as within the continental limits of the United States.[7] As Green pointed out, the 1942 law had proved "too complicated, time-consuming, and cumbersome to afford a genuine opportunity for voting" by the servicemen.[8]

In October Green submitted a new draft of the June proposal. It provided for the establishment of a War Ballot Commission of five members, at least two of them to be Democrats and two to be Republicans; all five members were to be appointed by the president and to be subject to Senate confirmation. Designed to function as a liaison between the various states and the federal government, the commission was to assume the responsibility for running the absentee voting procedure under the 1942 law. Among its duties, it was to expedite the airmailing of the federal ballots and to supply post cards requesting a state ballot instead of the proposed federal ballot. After the serviceman had been certified by an officer and had properly recorded his vote, the ballots were to be airmailed to the commission, which would in turn forward them to the appropriate state for inclusion in its electoral count. The Green-Lucas bill extended the federal ballot not only to servicemen outside of the United States but also to members of the merchant marine and to civilians attached to the armed forces overseas. Although the work of the commission was to be primarily administrative, to some the commission appeared to be assuming federal control of the voting system for servicemen, especially since the bill continued the suspension of the poll tax.[9]

The House Committee on Election of the President, Vice-President, and Representatives in Congress, under the chairmanship of Representative Worley, began its hearings on this and similar measures in October. Democratic National Chairman Frank Walker heartily endorsed the bill, but Republican National Committee Chairman Harrison E. Spangler believed that the method of selecting the War Ballot commissioners would too readily permit the president to control the commission by appointing a New Deal Democrat as the fifth commissioner. Southern Democrats John S. Gibson of Georgia and John E. Rankin, a white supremacist of Mississippi, vigorously attacked the entire bill as an outright invasion of states' rights.[10] Since four of the seven Democratic members from Mississippi, North Carolina, Alabama, and Georgia, as well as a majority of the five Republicans, were opposed to the bill on partisan grounds, the measure was effectively bottled up in the House committee.

Fortunately, a different political make-up characterized the Senate Committee on Privileges and Elections, of which Green was chairman. Liberal New Deal Democrats outnumbered the southerners, and the Republicans were willing to recommend passage of the bill with certain amendments to prevent Roosevelt from dominating the commission and its work. In mid-November 1943, with only two defections, Green's committee approved the bill for Senate action. To meet Republican objections, the committee recommended that the commission be composed of only four members, two Democrats and two Republicans, with the chief justice of the United States or another member of the Court chosen by the chief justice as a fifth member in the event of a tied vote. Although Green claimed that a tied vote would be highly unlikely, since the work of the commission would be almost entirely administrative, he agreed to the amendment in order to gain Republican support. A problem arose when Chief Justice Harlan Stone informed Senator Vandenberg that he would neither serve on the commission nor permit a member of the Court to do so, because he considered such service incompatible with the proper role and function of the Court. Since Green had declared earlier that the work of the commission would be primarily administrative, he could hardly oppose Vandenberg's proposal of a four-member commission, which he accepted as an amendment to the bill.[11]

Having gained this point, Republican Senate leaders proposed further amendments. Senator Styles Bridges of New Hampshire led the fight to require the president to draw the commissioners from lists submitted by the Republican and Democratic national committees. The Republicans assumed that Roosevelt would select moderate or liberal members of their party, so that the commission would be under his own control. Some Republicans even believed that FDR would manipulate the mailing, handling, and validation of ballots to ensure victory for himself in 1944. Recommendation by the Republican National Committee would ensure that only solid members of that party could be nominated to the commission; Bridges openly stated that his proposal was designed to keep Roosevelt from appointing Republicans with New Deal sympathies. Arguing that the Constitution gave the president the widest latitude in choosing appointees—who, however, had to be confirmed by the Senate—Green opposed the restriction Bridges proposed for members of the War Ballot Commission. Furthermore, Green said, to require the selection of nominees from party lists would reflect on the integrity of the president. Senators Green, Lucas, Barkley, and Hatch offered to vote against any Republican nominee to the commission who was unacceptable to the minority leadership if the Bridges proposal were dropped. When the vote was taken, a 33–33 tie prevented passage of the amendment; five Democrats had joined the twenty-eight Republicans in the attempt to limit the president's right of choice.[12]

The following day, however, a motion was narrowly passed to reconsider the vote. Three additional Democrats, among them Peter G. Gerry of Rhode Island, joined the Republicans in approving the amendment and excluding from the provisions of the bill civilians who worked overseas for the armed forces. With the assistance of Majority Leader Alben Barkley, Green and Lucas attempted to parry the proposal of C. Wayland Brooks, Republican of Illinois, to eliminate merchant seamen from the bill. According to Brooks, merchant seamen, because of their inordinately high salaries and the leftist tendencies of their leaders, did not deserve special treatment. An impassioned defense of the merchant marine by Claude Pepper, Democrat of Florida, and Green brought about the defeat of Brooks's amendment, 40 to 35. Green derived scant comfort from this single victory, for he was pessimistic about the future of his absentee voting bill.[13]

Although the Republicans had eliminated civilians from the voting bill, they decided to add a provision to include members of the Red Cross and the Society of Friends who were serving overseas in a civilian capacity. Not to be outdone by this request of Senator George D. Aiken of Vermont, Green asked for the addition as well of members of the Women's Auxiliary Ferry Service, the Women's Air Force Service Pilots, and the United Service Organizations who were entertaining troops both in the United States and overseas. The Senate approved this bipartisan padding of the bill by a majority of 52 to 21.[14]

Senator Robert A. Taft, the formidable Republican from Ohio, determined to prevent Roosevelt from using his executive position and his role as military leader to propagandize the servicemen, proposed that the absentee voting bill carry a set of provisions forbidding dissemination of political information to the servicemen by government officials. Normal communications from home, as well as books and magazines, were not included in the prohibition, which was to be interpreted liberally. While Taft intended simply to prohibit actual political propagandizing, the amendment was potentially repressive because of the danger of its rules being applied too vigorously by the military. Despite Lucas's unsuccessful attempts to exclude the army and navy from Taft's propaganda curbs, the amendment was passed as proposed, 42 to 35.[15]

The strongest opposition to the Green-Lucas bill came from the southern Democrats, led by Senator James O. Eastland and his fellow senator from Mississippi, Theodore G. Bilbo. Eastland made no attempt to hide his disdain for Negroes and other minority groups, and set out to defeat the Green-Lucas bill on the grounds that it was a thoroughly unconstitutional invasion of the right of the states to determine the qualifications of their own electorate. Such legislation, he maintained, would send carpetbaggers into the South, enfranchise people who had no right to be voters, and "destroy the sacred principle of the control of each state over its own election machinery and the right of the State to define the qualifications of its electors."[16] While Rankin, his colleague from Mississippi, stalled the House version in committee, Eastland attempted to redraft the bill completely in the Senate.

He submitted an amendment to the Green-Lucas bill that was in effect a substitute for it, since his proposal would have left all the machinery for absentee voting in the hands of the states. Overseas servicemen were included, but the War and Navy Departments were no longer to distribute the post card requests for ballots. Although the suspension of payment of poll taxes by servicemen was retained, state control of the machinery made a mockery of the provision. Just as the Senate was ready to vote on the amended Green-Lucas bill, Eastland attempted to substitute his own version. The soldiers' vote was not the issue, Eastland declared, but rather "whether we are to turn the election machinery of the country over to an aggregation of power-crazy bureaucrats in Washington . . . whether we are to permit expanding Federal power to destroy the States of the country."[17] Senators McClellan and McKellar, cosponsors of the substitute bill, joined the attack, and all three called the Green-Lucas bill unconstitutional. Green maintained that under the exigencies of war the Constitution could be stretched to permit the federal government to facilitate the voting procedures of the states and that the federal government would not supersede the states. Eastland and his colleagues from Arkansas and Tennessee contended, on the other hand, that only the states had the constitutional right to determine voter qualifications and that the federal government could not set aside any provision for absentee voting, no matter how intricate. Passage of the Absentee Voting Act of 1942, said Eastland, was no justification for this new proposal. When the vote was taken on the substitute bill, twenty-four Democrats, including all the southerners, joined with eighteen Republicans to pass the Eastland version. Once again Senator Gerry was in opposition to his fellow Rhode Islander. Aligned with Green and Lucas were twenty-five northern Democrats and twelve Republicans, including Vandenberg and Taft. The only element of the original Green-Lucas bill that remained was its number, S. 1285.[18]

Reactions to the coup varied widely. Senator Joseph Guffey of Pennsylvania, who had attacked the Eastland substitute as an "unholy alliance" of southern Democrats and Republicans under the leadership of Joseph Pew of Pennsylvania, further termed the bill "the most colossal vote steal in history."[19] Sidney Hillman, the chairman of the Political Action Committee of the CIO called Eastland's measure "cynical, brutal, and scandalous."[20] Ailing Senator Carter Glass of Virginia wrote Scott Lucas that the original bill was neither unconstitutional nor detrimental to the security and sovereignty of the states. If the Senate reconsidered the issue, Glass asked to be paired for the original Green-Lucas wording.[21]

The issue was by no means dead. In mid-December 1943 twenty-three Democratic and two Republican Representatives—left-wingers, according to Rankin—denounced the Eastland version as "a substitution for democracy" and a "slap in the face" to members of the armed forces.[22] Worley, holding the Eastland bill in his House committee, tried to work out a compromise, but the conservative coalition of southern Democrats and Republicans was too powerful. In January 1944, shortly after the Christmas recess, Rankin joined two other southerners and four Republicans in voting the Eastland version of S. 1285 out of the House committee, 7 to 5. Democratic Majority Leader John W. McCormack deplored the action of the committee, and Worley issued a minority report to the House in which he cited the need for, and defended the constitutionality of, the federal ballot.[23] Rankin, certain that he had enough votes to assure passage of the Eastland substitute, berated Worley for his liberal views, which he claimed would have "rung the death knell" of the Constitution and the Republic.[24]

Several of the states began to respond to agitation for a system to permit servicemen to vote. As chairman of the Senate Privileges and Elections Committee, Green had requested reports from the forty-eight governors on the status of their absentee voting laws; according to the forty-one replies, ten of the states considered their laws adequate or did not contemplate revising them, seventeen were awaiting congressional action, and fourteen were either holding sessions to consider new laws or making plans to do so. *Stars and Stripes*, the official servicemen's newspaper, reported that overseas soldiers were not only interested in casting their ballots in the coming election but that the closer they were to the fighting front the more eager they seemed to be to vote. This report sharply contrasted with the opinion of Admiral William F. Halsey that only "one in 500 [was] interested in voting."[25]

Despite the fact that the bill in the House still bore their names—or perhaps because it did—Green and Lucas introduced a new bill (S. 1612) into the Senate to provide for absentee servicemen's voting. on 11 January 1944 they proposed a United States War Ballot Commission composed of two Democrats and two Republicans chosen by the president from a list of six nominees submitted by the Democratic and Republican national committees and confirmed by the Senate. The commission was to consult with the War and Navy Departments and with the War Shipping Administration on the transfer of war ballots from servicemen to the commission and then to the individual states. It was a simple bill that cut much of the red tape from the original S. 1285 and presented the federal ballot once again as a supplement to the state ballot for states that maintained absentee voting laws. Again it provided for the suspension of poll taxes and state personal registration requirements. And as a sop to congressional states' righters, the new Green-Lucas bill withheld from the commission the power to rule on the validity of the ballots once they were marked by the servicemen and in the hands of state officials; this was left to the individual states, making it easy for recalcitrant state and local canvassers to discriminate against a federal ballot.[26]

By this time, however, the southerners had decided to attempt to negate the effects of the provisions suspending the poll tax and personal registration by supporting the Eastland substitute, which kept complete control of the absentee voting system in the hands of the states. Because of its provision permitting servicemen to vote by party preference while not requiring that candidates' names be written in, the new bill was derided as an outright attempt to carry the election for Roosevelt by encouraging straight ticket voting. One columnist claimed that the bill would "tammanyize the election" and deprive the states of their constitutional rights to determine which of their citizens should enjoy the privilege of casting a ballot.[27]

Like S. 1285, Green's and Lucas's S. 1612 was reported favorably out of Green's Committee on Privileges and Elections, with only two dissenting, Republican votes. Vandenberg told the Senate that since the states were making some attempt to update their laws and deal with the problem, Congress ought to defer action on the new Green-Lucas bill. Lucas, however, insisted that the federal government must become a vital cog in the election machinery, since the postal system could not handle both the voluminous state ballots and morale-building V-mail. When Taft claimed that the army and navy favored federal rather than state ballots because Secretaries Stimson and Knox (both Republicans) were "working for a fourth term," Lucas denounced the charge as "purely political poppycock of the highest type," adding that he was tired of the fourth term issue's being linked with attempts by him and Green to obtain a federal ballot for the fighting men and women throughout the world. Indeed, he warned that if the Republicans kept up their opposition to such a ballot, they would ensure a Democratic sweep of the 1944 elections and unwittingly hand Roosevelt a fourth term.[28]

The federal government, Green argued, had drafted the servicemen and suspended the taxes they would ordinarily have had to pay; therefore, the federal government should be able to suspend the poll tax for them, as well as the requirement that they register personally to vote. Moreover, he added, his proposal was devised solely to improve the mechanics of the Absentee Voting Act of 1942, which had given the servicemen the right to vote, and to facilitate their doing so. Green re-emphasized that he did not intend to deprive the states of their right to determine the qualifications of voters. He pointed out that servicemen should be able to vote by party preference because war conditions might make it impossible to learn the names of candidates for Congress. It was, he said, impractical to depend on the states' systems alone:

Illinois, for example, had 102 different kinds of ballots, each dependent on a single election district, and Maine elected its members of Congress in September rather than in November.[29]

As commander-in-chief Roosevelt had been reluctant to speak out, but on 26 January 1944 he finally sent a special message to Congress on wartime voting, urging the legislators to reject Eastland's substitute measure and to pass the new Green-Lucas bill. Terming the Eastland substitute a "meaningless bill" and a "fraud on the soldiers and sailors and marines now in training and fighting for us and our sacred rights," Roosevelt called voting one of the sacred rights and said that the federal ballot was imperative for men and women in the armed forces as well as for members of the merchant marine. If the Congress failed to make provisions for a federal ballot, the president went on, it would be outright discrimination against the armed forces. "Every member of the two Houses of Congress ought to be willing in justice 'to stand up and be counted,' " he declared.[30]

These harsh words from the president prompted Taft to denounce him for "meddling in legislative matters" and to describe the message as the official announcement of Roosevelt's candidacy for a fourth term. Taft contended that ten million servicemen "are to be marched up to the polls, just as the W.P.A. workers were marched to the polls in some of the elections in the past . . . handed a bobtail Federal ballot, with no names on it, and they are to be told in effect, 'Vote this ballot.' "[31] Taft went on to link the whole plan with the CIO's efforts to secure a fourth term for Roosevelt; the wartime voting procedure desired by Roosevelt, Green, and Lucas was, in Taft's view, an "effort to wipe out this Congress" and a means to "subordinate the Congress to the Executive."

The day after Roosevelt's message, Green inserted into the *Congressional Record* a long memorandum on the constitutionality of a federal ballot. Once again, he based his argument on the wartime powers of the government. Registration for voting was a "procedural requirement" and a "condition," as distinguished from a "qualification," for voting. The poll tax was a "tax" and not a "means of classifying voters on the basis of financial stability."[32]

In the House, Rankin continued to work for House passage of the committee-approved bill, which was now commonly referred to as the Eastland-Rankin substitute. Calling the new Green-Lucas bill an attempt to propose "an April-fool ballot," Rankin led the House in defeating, 233 to 160, its supporters' request for a roll-call vote on the measure on 1 February. With this victory on record, Rankin was now certain of carrying his point and could afford a roll-call vote on Worley's companion bill to the Green-Lucas proposal. The vote was taken, and Worley's bill was defeated, 224 to 168. Convinced that nothing better could be passed, the House adopted the Eastland-Rankin substitute, 328 to 69, on 3 February 1944.[33]

The fight still raged in the Senate. The amendment, proposed by Democrat John H. Overton of Louisiana, to repeal suspension of the poll tax and of personal registration was overwhelmingly defeated, 69 to 16. Since only the southern Democrats could afford outright opposition to that provision, Senator Taft and five other Republicans, supported by nine southern Democrats, then proposed a compromise that would have applied the provisions of a federal ballot only when a state with no workable system of its own requested that the federal ballot principle be applied to the state's election system during wartime. In addition, voting would be by name only, not by party preference, and state qualifications would prevail in all instances.[34]

Green and Lucas were determined not to yield any more than was absolutely necessary. Urged to continue the fight by the governor of Rhode Island, J. Howard McGrath, who preferred to have the federal government bear the expense of an absentee voting system, Green fully understood the importance of the final version of the bill—especially since the Democratic party in his own state needed the servicemen's votes. Not only did most of the senator's mail at this time support his position for a federal ballot, but the National Association for the Advancement of Colored People informed him that its membership of 250,000, angered and dismayed at the "collaboration of Republicans with the Eastland-Rankin bloc," was "unreservedly for the Green-Lucas bill and against any so-called states rights measures."[35] When Taft's compromise was put to a vote in the Senate on 4 February, Green and Lucas, with the help of nine Republicans and LaFollette, a Progressive, mustered enough votes to defeat it, 46 to 42.[36] Vandenberg salvaged the one part of the Taft proposal with which he agreed, however, and persuaded the Senate to approve unanimously the provision requiring that the names of the candidates rather than party preferences be written on the ballot.[37] Green and Lucas managed to abort an attempt to set aside their bill and take up the House-passed Eastland-Rankin substitute. A few days later, however, the Senate voted to suspend debate temporarily on the Green-Lucas proposal and to vote on the Eastland-Rankin measure. (It was necessary to vote again because the form of the substitute differed slightly from the version passed by the House.) On 8 February the Senate debated the substitute, to which the Green-Lucas forces added their proposals in the form of an amendment to the Eastland-Rankin version; an amendment was also inserted to guarantee a federal ballot to servicemen should a state ballot not reach them in time to be cast in the election. The addition was made as part of a complicated parliamentary maneuver engineered by Majority Leader Barkley to bring the problem to a Senate-House conference committee, so that the differences among the various factions could be resolved. Barkley led a move in the Senate to pass the new Green-Lucas bill, making a House-Senate conference essential.[38]

The selection of the conferees was itself a problem. Ordinarily when two different versions of a bill must be reconciled in conference, the conferees are the principal members of the committees that originally considered the bills. In this case, however, opinion was divided not only between the congressional bodies but also within each body, ranging from that held by the states' righters to that of the advocates of the federal ballot. To be as fair as possible, the House chose two legislators who supported the federal ballot and three who opposed it, and the Senate chose three, including Green, who supported it and two who were in opposition. Green led the Senate conferees, and Rankin led those from the House.[39]

With five supporters and five opponents, the conferees were deadlocked for two weeks. They held seven meetings, proposed a wide variety of compromises, but failed to come to an agreement. On 1 March 1944 the members of the Conference Committee on Absentee Wartime Voting finally reached a compromise that had a strong states' rights flavor and limited the federal ballot to servicemen who came from states without machinery for absentee voting (actually only two) and to servicemen who had requested, but had not received, a state ballot by 1 October. Furthermore, use of the federal ballot was denied to servicemen stationed within the continental limits of the United States. Another provision required not only that the governor of a state certify that the federal ballot was acceptable but also that the laws of his state so specify. Finding this provision completely unacceptable, Green declared that he would vote against the conference compromise on the Senate floor and that he hoped Roosevelt would veto the bill if it were passed. The advantages of the bill were now outweighed by its disadvantages in Green's opinion, since it appeared likely that even fewer than the twenty-eight thousand service personnel who had voted in 1942 would be able to vote under the new bill. No bill at all was better than one that made it harder rather than easier for the servicemen to vote, especially since administration of the voting procedure had in effect been turned over to the states by eliminating the independent War Ballot Commission. Also, even though the provisions suspending the poll tax and eliminating the personal registration requirement had been retained, there was no guarantee that these two principles would have any effect if the ballots had to be validated and certified by the states. Green and Lucas were thus totally opposed to the bill that bore their names, and Green turned the floor management of the committee-approved compromise over to Senator Thomas Connally of Texas.[40]

On 13 March 1944 Green made a last, unsuccessful fight against passage of the bill, arguing that it was a travesty to supply a federal ballot only to overseas personnel, that the deadlines written into the measure would make it almost impossible for servicemen to vote, and that if Congress passed the bill, it would relegate to the states "a matter over which it had both the right and the duty to legislate itself."[41] In spite of these arguments, the Senate approved the compromise bill, 47 to 31, and the House passed it, 273 to 111.[42] A presidential veto seemed almost certain until half of the states informed Roosevelt that they would not readjust their state laws to permit the governors to certify use of the federal ballot; the president then permitted the bill to become law without his signature, after the constitutional ten-day waiting period. At the same time, he sent a message to the Congress, asking for the passage of a more liberal law in time for the 1944 election, preferably one providing for distribution of federal ballots even when servicemen had not requested them.[43]

On 1 April 1944, after the president's message, Green and Lucas introduced another bill.[44] Its fate was largely determined by southern anger over the Supreme Court's decision, in *Smith* v. *Allwright,* that a primary was constitutionally part of the election process. The so-called white primary law of Texas—and therefore those of other southern states—was ruled contrary to the Fourteenth Amendment of the Constitution. This 8 to 1 decision greatly increased southern bitterness over liberal attempts to ease voting restrictions, and Senator Burnet Maybank of South Carolina vowed that the South would protect its white primaries. "Regardless of any Supreme Court decisions and any laws that may be passed by Congress, we of the South," said Maybank, "will maintain our political and social institutions as we believe to be in the best interest of our people."[45]

As it stood, then, the Absentee Voting Act of 1944 specified that: (1) A member of the armed forces stationed in the United States had to use a state ballot if his home state had absentee voting laws; in a state not having such a law, the federal ballot was permissible only if the governor certified that the federal ballot was authorized by state law. (2) A member of the armed forces outside the United States could use a federal ballot only if he had applied for a state ballot by 1 September and had not received it by 1 October; even under these circumstances, the governor of the soldier's home state had to certify that state laws permitted the federal ballot to be used. (3) Free airmail service was to be provided for both state and federal ballots. (4) The War and Navy Departments and the Maritime Commission were to assist the states in sending ballots to servicemen and in returning them. (5) The voting provisions were to extend to the Merchant Marine, the Red Cross, the Society of Friends, the United Service Organizations, and the Women's Auxiliary Service Pilots. (6) The Taft restrictions on the distribution of political material to members of the armed forces were to be observed.

Taft's amendment almost immediately caused difficulties, for the War Department, so as not to be accused of giving political support to the administration, interpreted restrictions on the political propaganda overzealously. For instance, war correspondents in Italy were warned against polling soldiers on their political views; distribution to soldiers overseas of a movie about Woodrow Wilson was prohibited as a possible indication of support for the Democratic party; and British newspapers and magazines were banned from American bases in Britain until after the election because they reported the campaign in the United States. The Army even barred Charles A. Beard's *Republic* and

Catherine Drinker Bowen's *Yankee from Olympus,* a biography of Oliver Wendell Holmes, on the grounds that the books were somewhat complimentary to Franklin D. Roosevelt.[46] Green exploited several such ridiculous situations.

To ease military political restrictions, Green introduced a bill in the Senate to give the two major parties equal time on government-controlled overseas radio for political speeches, to permit dissemination of civilian publications overseas, to remove restrictions on servicemen's publications like *Stars and Stripes,* and to allow political communications to be mailed to a serviceman if addressed to him personally. When Green's Committee on Privileges and Elections reported the bill out favorably, even Taft stated that he agreed fully with its provisions. It was unanimously passed by the Senate on 22 August 1944.[47]

After Roosevelt swept to victory in 1944 in his fourth-term bid for the presidency, it was difficult to separate civilian from military ballots in order to measure the impact of the absentee voting of servicemen. Of 2,691,160 military ballots received by state officials in the election, only 84,835 were federal supplementary ballots (only twenty states had made provisions for their use). In Colorado, Maryland, New Jersey, Pennsylvania, and Rhode Island, which counted military ballots separately from civilian ballots, Roosevelt won the military vote by a 3 to 2 ratio. In New York City, which also maintained a separate count, FDR received 72.6 per cent of the 242,082 military ballots cast. In Rhode Island, Roosevelt enjoyed a 2 to 1 majority of the 23,000 votes cast there. Although the servicemen's vote had favored Roosevelt, it had not been as crucial as it had been expected to be, because of FDR's strong plurality.[48]

Approximately 30 per cent of the nine million eligible men and women in the armed forces voted by absentee ballot in 1944. Although the original Green-Lucas bill was not passed in the form that its sponsors had desired, their insistence in bringing the matter before the Congress and the country had generated increased interest in absentee servicemen's voting; as a result, most of the states made some provision for an absentee state ballot. If the widely scattered service population and the difficulties involved in implementing service voting are taken into account, 30 per cent was a heartening proportion, especially since only 0.5 per cent had voted in 1942.[49] Although the war ended shortly thereafter and with it the need for the legislation, Green had the satisfaction of knowing that he not only had raised an important issue but also had done his best to right a wrong.

5. Politician

EXPEDIENCY and choice require a United States senator to play many political roles. As a representative of his state he must maintain cordial relations with the state party, but he is also responsible to the national party. While Theodore Francis Green frequently supported President Roosevelt against the advice of his more vocal constituents, the senator never forgot his political colleagues in Rhode Island, especially in matters of patronage.

During his twenty-four years in the Senate, Green, with the assistance of Edward J. Higgins, balanced his responsibility to Rhode Island with his conception of the best interests of the nation. He campaigned tirelessly for Roosevelt, as much for ideological reasons as for practical ones. In his own campaigns for re-election to the Senate, Green tended to run against the Republican party as a whole rather than against his opponent as a person. Throughout his Senate career, he was fortunate in having Higgins's advice and aid in dealing with Rhode Island personalities, for nothing that took place on the local political scene escaped the vigilant Higgins. The decisions, however, were always Green's; Higgins never tried to force his own views on Green.

A freshman senator often finds it useful to hire Capitol Hill professionals as members of his staff to help him become familiar with the intricate procedures of the Senate. But when he set up his Washington office in 1937, Green employed only personnel from his Rhode Island gubernatorial staff. Its key member was Higgins, who had been Green's personal secretary during his four years as governor. As Green's administrative assistant in Washington, Higgins ruled the senator's office with a firm hand, never wavering from the principle that only Rhode Island Democrats whose loyalty to Green was assured were to be employed.

The relationship between the Yankee patrician and Higgins was singularly productive. A tough, shrewd Irish Catholic from a small Rhode Island town who had scores of friends in state and local politics, Higgins had a remarkably incisive mind and an uncanny ability to assess the situation within the state. The personalities of the two men were as different as their tastes: while Green would spend hours poring over his collection of Chinese scrolls, Higgins enjoyed nothing more than watching a baseball game. Their social contacts were as dissimilar as their backgrounds and interests. They shared, however, an unwavering loyalty to the Democratic party and a deep respect for each other. Their political familiarity never bred contempt, and few ill-humored words ever passed between them. Green gave Higgins a free hand in choosing personnel and running his office, although every appointment and all important decisions were cleared with the senator.

Higgins never took advantage of his unique position. In time he became an effective intermediary between Green and other senators. For example, Higgins developed close ties with the staff of Senator Lyndon B. Johnson; when Johnson subsequently became majority leader, Higgins made effective use of his access to the Democratic leader. Senators, as well as staff aides, knew that Green's assistant was trustworthy and that he spoke with Green's authority behind him. As one prominent southern Democrat put it, "Higgins played the ideal role. He was loyal as any Senator could ask and a good deal smarter than most of us."[1] When a visiting Rhode Islander arrived in Washington to seek a favor, an introduction to an agency, or advice, he had only to go to Higgins. In Senator John O. Pastore's words, "You just didn't have to go any further than Eddie. Eddie handled it for you."[2]

With these capacities and responsibilities, it is hardly surprising that Higgins initiated most of the patronage appointments. Although the patronage system has been often condemned by reformers, it can be cogently argued that it is beneficial to a democratic political system; that by rewarding competence and loyalty, politicians have brought many capable people into government service who would not otherwise have entered it. In any case, Higgins and Green were able to open doors for the promising, bright, and ambitious. Washington, Higgins once informed a Rhode Island recipient of Green's patronage, was "playing ball one hundred per cent with the Senator"; because Green was the only New England senator supporting FDR's Court plan, it was "no trouble at all to get over an appointment."[3]

Soon after he arrived in Washington, Green made many appointments through his initial committee assignments. As a new member of the Post Offices and Roads Committee, the senator from Rhode Island informed the chairman of the committee, Senator Kenneth McKellar of Tennessee, that all nominations for postmasters in Rhode Island were to be cleared by Green personally.[4] Requests for new post office buildings and other federal projects came pouring into the senator's office from contractors, and demands for new mail carriers became so burdensome that Green finally was forced to shunt these requests to the Post Office Department for processing. Postal patronage was shared to some extent with the rest of the Rhode Island Democratic delegation to Congress, and even Senator Peter G. Gerry, despite his anti-Roosevelt stance, was given one or two positions to fill. For the most part, however, Higgins made certain that Green's office controlled the bulk of the appointments.[5]

Fewer opportunities for dispensing patronage were available to a member of the Senate Appropriations Committee than to a member of the Post Office Committee. Nevertheless, Green was able to place one man with the Capitol police. A Brown University economics professor was also appointed to the Social Security Board on Green's recommendation. And Robert C. Dunphy eventually became sergeant-at-arms of the Senate because Senator Carl Hayden of Arizona, as a favor to Green in 1955, used his influence to obtain the position of deputy sergeant-at-arms for Dunphy, a Rhode Islander. Ten years later the senior post became vacant, and Dunphy was chosen to fill it by the Democratic majority.[6]

An illuminating example of Higgins's role in the allotment of patronage can be seen in the appointment in 1946 of John Nicholas Brown as assistant secretary of the navy for air. Robert E. Hannegan, the postmaster general and chairman of the Democratic National Committee, informed Higgins and United States Solicitor General J. Howard McGrath that an appointment was pending and that they should nominate candidates immediately if they wanted the position to go to a Rhode Islander rather than to the Wall Street investment banker that Secretary of the Navy James Forrestal wanted to have appointed to the post. With McGrath's help, Higgins made up a short list of Rhode Island Democrats. Since Green was then officially visiting the aircraft carrier U.S.S. *Enterprise* off Cuba, Higgins assumed the responsibility for forwarding the list to Hannegan. When McGrath called at two o'clock the following morning to suggest Brown, a prominent Rhode Island Democrat and strong supporter of Senator Green, as a possible additional candidate, Higgins added Brown's name to the list; he also sent, over Green's signature, a letter to Truman recommending Brown. At the time neither Higgins nor the senator knew whether Brown was available for the position of assistant secretary; fortunately, the nominee expressed some interest when Higgins asked him. Senator Green flew to the Newport Naval Base from the *Enterprise* and was informed by a telephone call from Higgins in Washington that the appointment was imminent. Green immediately called the president and urged Brown's appointment because of his service to the party. Truman asked Brown to come to Washington the following morning, and ten days later the Rhode Islander was named assistant secretary of the navy for air. Green's persuasive intervention with Truman had overridden the recommendation of the secretary of the navy.[7]

Judgeships were another important source of patronage for the senator, who was under pressure from his Rhode Island senatorial colleague to prove that support of President Roosevelt was beneficial to Rhode Islanders. Since the Democrats had not fared well in the state in the 1938 elections, Green was anxious to solidify his position by demonstrating the strength of his influence with Roosevelt in matters of patronage. When a vacancy occurred in the First District Circuit Court of Appeals—despite some pressure to recommend Patrick Curran, his former law partner—Green urged the selection of John C. Mahoney, a Rhode Island Democrat and federal court judge; but Roosevelt, no doubt the recipient of equally fervent appeals from each of the states in the district, promoted Calvert Magruder of Massachusetts. Shortly after this disappointing development, another justice in the circuit court resigned, and Green again took up the battle. On this occasion his efforts were expended not only for Mahoney but also for John Hartigan, the Rhode Island Democratic party chairman who wanted to succeed to Mahoney's position. Because controversial neutrality legislation was being debated and Roosevelt did not want to jeopardize it by extraneous patronage squabbles, appointments were delayed for several months. Although Roosevelt assured Green that his recommendations would be considered in due course, the patronage issue was so crucial for Green that he requested from Senator Henry Ashurst, chairman of the Judiciary Committee, the names submitted by the president to fill the vacancy. Green, in short, fully intended to use "senatorial courtesy" to stop any appointment other than his own. The attorney general's office hastened to inform Green that no action would be taken on the appointment without Green's approval. On 11 January 1940 Roosevelt sent both Mahoney's and Hartigan's names to the Senate for confirmation of their appointments to the federal circuit and district courts, respectively. The nominees were confirmed in February, and a celebration was held after the swearing-in ceremonies at the end of the month.[8]

The power of a senator can often be used to punish as well as to reward. During his tenure as Rhode Island's governor, Green had been a determined opponent of efforts to legalize dog racing. The United States Marshal for Rhode Island, William Goucher, had incurred Green's enmity by his support of dog-racing interests. Goucher's commission, which paid $4,200 a year and involved as well the appointment of five deputy marshals, expired in January 1938. Green informed Roosevelt that he would not endorse Goucher's reappointment, although he would not oppose another federal appointment for the marshal, "preferably outside of Rhode Island." Copies of the senator's letter were sent to Attorney General Homer Cummings and to Postmaster General James A. Farley, who as chairman of the Democratic National Committee handled much of the president's patronage. Roosevelt did not reappoint Goucher, who subsequently received no other position from the party. To replace Goucher, Green recommended Neale Murphy, who, when Green was governor of Rhode Island, had been his chief clerk. Although other suggestions were made by prominent Rhode Island Democrats, Roosevelt appointed Murphy, giving Higgins the pleasant duty of overseeing the appointments of the five deputies. Two of the incumbents were reappointed, but the other three were replaced by individuals Higgins considered to be deserving, dependable Democrats.[9]

The patronage system is also commonly used to dispose of potential political opponents by appointing them to high office. When Democratic incumbent Governor Robert E. Quinn was defeated for re-election in 1938 by Republican William H. Vanderbilt, he became interested in running for the Senate. When the Congress established the Court of Military Appeals, Higgins and Green saw their opportunity and urged Quinn's appointment as the court's chief judge. Unable to resist the offer, Quinn was therefore eliminated from future battles for Green's Senate seat.

Unlike many who, having reached the United States Senate, consider themselves above political infighting within the state they represent, Senator Green, with the assistance of Higgins, continued to play a major role as senior Democratic politician in Rhode Island. In 1944, for instance, he used his influence to promote John O. Pastore of the state attorney general's office as the Democratic party's nominee for lieutenant governor.[10]

A new kind of patronage had become important during the 1930s. With thousands of constituents unable to find work, federal public works projects were a primary source of leverage; a politician who controlled scarce jobs could demand intense loyalty from his followers.

Like many states, Rhode Island tried to transfer maximum financial responsibility for depression relief programs to the federal government. But the Public Works Administration was not always easily tapped for funds. In 1937, for example, the federal government refused to pay for three projects Rhode Island considered essential to its economy. Senator Green and his aide were well aware of the political importance of obtaining the construction funds, and Green went directly to Roosevelt. The president, however, refused to support Green's request, and an appeal to Harold Ickes, secretary of the interior, was also futile.[11]

Fortunately, Green had greater success on other occasions. When federal plans for cutting back the development of Beach Pond in Washington County threatened to put 175 persons out of work, a great deal of pressure was brought to bear by the towns and by many civic groups in the county. The senator was so forceful and insistent with the Department of the Interior that funds were eventually allotted from the National Parks Service, and control of the project was given to the Work Projects Administration.

Even before Green went to the Senate, a plan to construct a bridge over Narragansett Bay between Jamestown and North Kingstown had been rejected as ineligible for federal funds. The government had argued that the costs of maintaining such a bridge could not be covered by anticipated tolls, but when Green arrived in Washington, he set his staff to work to convince WPA authorities that such a bridge was economically feasible and needed. In the end he overcame the agency's objections, and construction of the bridge was authorized in 1938 at a cost of $1.4 million.[12]

In the late 1930s Green also made a considerable effort to keep in Rhode Island the six Civilian Conservation Corps camps that had been established there. The national aim of the CCC was to bolster the economy and to provide young people with productive work that would help to conserve natural resources, but in Rhode Island as in other states there were political considerations as well. Higgins, for instance, wanted to make certain that Democrats who had supported Green and who needed jobs were provided for in the CCC camps. When, in March 1937, the army, which administered the camps, wanted to transfer the supervision of the CCC camp at Fort Adams in Newport to New London, Connecticut, or to Camp Devens, Massachusetts, Rhode Island Democrats feared that the assignment of professional people, such as doctors, would pass from their jurisdiction. Aside from the loss of political control, in 1935 the CCC had spent about $150,000 among fifty-two firms in Newport alone; in the rest of the state the CCC did business with more than a hundred other establishments. The director of Emergency Conservation Work, however, resisted all pleas and pressures; not only were the administrative changes made, but the government announced that two of the six camps were to be closed completely. Green was no more successful in saving the two camps than in preventing the administrative changes; by his constant harassment of federal officials including Secretary of Agriculture Henry A. Wallace, however, he made certain that the four remaining CCC camps remained operative until the entire program was ended in 1941.[13]

As war approached in Europe and Japan's intentions in the Pacific appeared more and more ominous, the United States reluctantly turned its attention to military preparedness. Federal funds were set aside to expand the pool of naval reserve officers by instituting naval training units in selected universities, and Brown University, from which Green had graduated in 1887, sought an NROTC unit. When the senator made inquiries for his alma mater at the Navy Department (he was on the Naval Affairs Subcommittee of the Senate Appropriations Committee), he was told that Brown would be considered if Congress allocated more money but that the university was not eligible for selection in 1939 because a formal application had not been received. By early 1940, when Brown's president, Henry M. Wriston, had finally obtained the consent of the university's governing body and was able to make a formal, late application, the Navy Department had established the new units only at Michigan and Oklahoma. Then Congress passed further appropriations for additional units, and the Rhode Island institution was one of eight universities and colleges assigned a naval training unit. Roosevelt himself had deleted Holy Cross from the list submitted to him and substituted Brown—in spite of the fact that isolationist Senator David I. Walsh of Massachusetts was chairman of the powerful Naval Affairs Committee.[14]

The navy, one of the largest employers in Rhode Island, and its affairs were of prime importance to the state's congressional delegation. The establishment of the naval air station at Quonset Point was one of the major accomplishments of Green's first term as senator. Retrenchment by the navy at Newport was one of the few issues that united Senator Green, who was on the Naval Affairs Subcommittee of the Senate Appropriations Committee, and Senator Gerry, who was a member of the Senate Naval Affairs Committee. And as the war became imminent, Green even traded influence with conservative Representative Ralph Brewster of Maine, who was the fourth-ranking Republican on the House Naval Affairs Committee.[15] The Navy Department was thus placed under considerable congressional pressure.

After President Roosevelt decided in 1938 to bolster the naval forces and Congress authorized an increase in the size of the navy, the president requested authorization and appropriations to develop twelve naval bases. A close friend of Higgins—Louis E. Denfeld, at that time a commander and administrative aide to the chief of naval operations, Admiral William D. Leahy—told Higgins that an Office of Naval Operations survey of coastal areas indicated that Quonset Point would be an excellent site for a new naval air station and carrier base. Although both Senator Walsh of Massachusetts and Senator Robert F. Wagner of New York were anxious to secure the proposed base for their states, Green was especially eager to be credited with bringing it to Rhode Island because Walsh was an ally of Senator Gerry, who Green believed was spreading rumors impugning his ability to secure benefits for Rhode Island.[16]

Green was advised by Roosevelt, to whom he went with the information provided by Denfeld, to arrange for the acquisition of state land for a base; Assistant Secretary of the Navy Edison, however, told Green that although the navy would accept the land for a possible base, no commitment could be made until Congress enacted legislation authorizing construction of the base. Governor Vanderbilt would have much preferred to work through his fellow Republicans, Rhode Island's two United States representatives, Charles F. Risk and Harry Sandager, but they had little influence in Washington; indeed, Sandager had incurred the wrath of the navy for his vehement opposition to expansion of the naval base at Guam.[17] Vanderbilt was therefore compelled to work closely with Green, who had access to Roosevelt and influence with the Navy Department. When the governor informed the senator that the Rhode Island legislature would agree to give the land to the federal government if the navy would guarantee that the base would be built on it, Green replied that the faster the land was ceded, the faster Congress would act. On 5 April 1939, the state relinquished the land.[18]

Green had introduced an amendment to the naval construction bill of 1938 to authorize $1 million for the acquisition of private land to supplement the land given by the state. Roosevelt himself made the decision that the naval base was to be constructed at Quonset. And while the Senate Naval Affairs Committee was dealing with the Green amendment, copies of the Rhode Island resolution granting the land to the federal government arrived in Washington. As soon as funds were finally appropriated in May 1939, the navy began to acquire large tracts of land (through realtors suggested by Higgins) for additions to the Quonset base and for the Seabee base at Davisville, Rhode Island.[19]

Green next set to work to obtain an appropriation of $25 million for the construction of the base by introducing an authorization bill. As soon as the construction money for the base was appropriated by Congress in May 1940, Rhode Island contractors descended on Higgins for their share of the windfall, and when Senator Gerry recommended as consulting construction engineers a firm other than the one Senator Green preferred, Green reminded the president of Gerry's opposition to New Deal legislation and of his own support. On Roosevelt's recommendation the Navy Department awarded the contract to the Maguire Company, which Green favored. However, although a Newport firm received a $400,000 contract to build mess halls, the Navy Department awarded the major construction contract to the George A. Fuller Company of New York. With Higgins, on the one hand, actively striving to obtain positions for as many Democrats as possible, and Governor Vanderbilt, on the other, working equally hard for the Republicans, President Roosevelt had to intervene personally. A promise was extracted from Lou R. Crandall, president of the Fuller Company, to subcontract to Rhode Island manufacturers and wholesalers whenever possible, and Higgins supplied Crandall with a list of forty-three firms for that purpose. The Rhode Island Democrats had to be content with whatever they could get, although it was less than they had hoped for.[20]

As the base neared completion in 1941, the *Providence Journal* welcomed it as a permanent establishment and a "part of the life of Rhode Island." In January 1939, however, the *Journal* had declared that Green's land acquisition legislation placed "pork-barrel psychology above considerations of priority in providing for the common defense." Green was quick to have the two editorials inserted side by side in the *Congressional Record*.[21]

Always known as a prolabor Democrat, in 1937 Green found himself involved as a senator with the problems of the unions that represented the civilian machinists employed at the Naval Torpedo Station at Newport. According to the unions, the naval officers in charge of the station were engaged not only in anti-union activity but, worse yet, in anti-Democratic agitation. Urged to use his influence to ensure that the next commander of the station would be an officer better able to get along with the three thousand civilian employees, Green wrote to Assistant Secretary of the Navy Charles Edison, charging that several civilians had been demoted because of their union activities. Edison denied the charge, but complaints of harassment by the officers continued to reach Green. They were especially vexing to Higgins, for one of the union's primary targets was the base's chief ordnance officer, a friend who had helped to place Rhode Island Democrats on the bidding list of suppliers of parts and material.

The president of the International Machinists' Union at Newport, Harold Kingsley, even requested that Green oppose this officer's promotion to flag rank.[22]

There was some truth to the charges that several naval and civilian executives were outspoken enemies of organized labor and had attempted to suppress labor union activity at Newport. Finally Senator Green met with twenty union representatives at Newport on 5 November 1938. At his suggestion a petition setting forth the union's complaints was drawn up by Kingsley and presumably signed by many of the union leaders. Green had intended to present this document personally to FDR, but Roosevelt had gone to Warm Springs; Green therefore forwarded it to Georgia, where, after reviewing two of the cases that the union claimed showed discrimination against their members, the president concluded that the union's charges were unwarranted.[23]

At this point several union men whose names had appeared on the petition complained to Higgins that their names had been forged. Higgins, whom Green sent to Newport to investigate, discovered that there had indeed been misrepresentation, apparently motivated by a desire to retaliate against proposed expansion of naval stations in Virginia or on the West Coast rather than at Newport. Green immediately informed Roosevelt, who ordered a Civil Service Commission investigation into the case. The union rid itself of Kingsley, and after this episode Green was much more cautious about accepting union complaints.[24]

In 1937, too, the Rhode Island congressional delegation began to urge the navy to expand and modernize the Newport base instead of carrying out plans for manufacturing torpedos in Alexandria, Virginia. The navy opposed further expansion of the Newport torpedo facility because it was deemed too small and outdated, but Assistant Secretary of the Navy Edison assured Green and Gerry that the Newport station would not be closed or reduced, although he was adamant about the need to build other facilities elsewhere. Green took the matter up with Roosevelt, who told him in a memorandum that he believed that torpedos should be manufactured in Virginia as well as Newport to avoid putting all of the country's eggs in one basket. Roosevelt promised, however, that Newport would not be superseded and that its torpedo factory would be sufficiently modernized to put it on a par with other leading military establishments. Green circulated Roosevelt's memorandum among Newport businessmen, unions, and civic leaders as evidence that Newport would not be hurt by the expansion of any other facility.[25]

Roosevelt, Green said, had also promised to spend the $2 million the senator had recommended for new buildings and machinery at Newport. The navy, on the other hand, declared that it would allot only $300,000 for new machinery and tools.[26] In any case, when the war broke out, all navy bases on the mainland, among them those at Newport and Alexandria, were expanded substantially, and Green saw to it as a member of the Naval Affairs Subcommittee that Newport received its share of the vast sums appropriated. Not only was a training base for naval recruits established there, but the Naval War College was expanded as well. So persuasive was Green that in a Senate-House conference committee ironing out differences in an appropriations bill he once managed to retain increases for Newport despite reductions for bases in California, Illinois, New York, and Maryland. The Rhode Island senator claimed that his success was "additional evidence that it pays to be in attendance at committee meetings" and to learn all the details of bills.[27]

When the war ended, the Navy Department reviewed its need for torpedoes in the light of changing weapons systems. A report made at the direction of Lewis L. Strauss, assistant to the secretary of the navy, found the Newport facilities and base too inefficient to continue carrying heavy responsibility for the manufacture of torpedoes. Secretary of the Navy Forrestal therefore informed Green that while Newport would continue to conduct research and to overhaul torpedoes, manufacturing facilities would be expanded at Forest Park, Illinois. In spite of the Rhode Island congressional delegation's protest, President Truman backed the navy decision on the grounds that Forest Park was a modern, fully equipped plant that was, unlike Newport, readily expandable in case of war and more militarily secure. Green held Lewis Strauss responsible for the decision and years later, in January 1959, was among those who voted against Strauss, 49 to 46, after he had been nominated as secretary of commerce by President Eisenhower.[28]

In an attempt to force a reversal of the decision against Newport, Green and Representative Forand used the 1947 navy appropriations bill as their instrument. In the House Forand introduced an amendment to the bill forbidding the use of any of the funds appropriated "for the manufacture, assembly, repair, or overhaul of torpedoes at the Naval Ordnance Plant, Forest Park, Illinois." Forand was supported by several New England congressmen on both sides of the aisle, and the amendment was agreed upon and included in the bill. Testimony in the hearings on the bill held by the Senate Appropriations Subcommittee on Naval Affairs made it clear that the navy fully intended to close the Newport factory in favor of Forest Park, and the subcommittee voted to retain the Forand amendment. When, however, the full Appropriations Committee deleted it, Green made a last ditch effort on the floor of the Senate. Senator Scott Lucas of Illinois argued against Green, claiming that his own state offered better facilities than Rhode Island and that Green wanted the Newport base maintained because of nostalgia for the past. In spite of Green's and Gerry's stout defense of Newport, an attempt to attach the Forand amendment to the bill on the floor of the Senate was defeated, 28 to 26. Left in the bill, however, was a Green amendment appropriating $350,000 to put the Newport facility in operating condition on a standby basis.[29]

The closing of the torpedo factory had a serious impact on a number of civilian employees. Between 250 and 300 men had served twenty-five years or more at the base but were not entitled to any civil service retirement benefits. Green proposed that all involuntarily retired civil service employees with twenty-five years of service be pensioned off, provided they had also reached the age of fifty-five. This proposal would have provided for some, but not all, of the employees who were victims of the navy's decision. A similar bill, but without an age limitation, was introduced into the House by Representative Aime Forand and passed in July 1946. Forand's bill was substituted for the Green bill in the Senate, but in a conference committee the Senate insisted on keeping the age limitation, thus cutting off without pensions about 130 men from Newport who were under fifty-five years of age but who had served for twenty-five years. The only hope for these men rested in another bill introduced by Green that deleted the age limitation but applied the retirement plan only to those dismissed between 1 July 1945 and 30 June 1947. This provision was intended to make the measure more palatable to the Senate, because it would affect only the 130 men at Newport and not all civil service employees. The Senate Committee on Civil Service, however, reinserted the age limitation, and the bill died when Congress passed the conference committee-amended Forand bill.[30]

During the next two years Green vainly proposed several bills to help the dismissed Newport employees. By 1947, however, because of the cold war, the Navy began to use Newport as a main operating base, more than doubling the number of vessels stationed there, causing an influx of servicemen and their dependents, and drastically increasing employment. In 1949 a bill proposed by a California congressman concerned about retirement problems in West Coast navy yards was substituted for another of Green's bills. This measure, which gave more liberal retirement benefits with fewer requirements, was finally passed, and

Green worked hard for its enactment; he was "more interested in having it passed for the benefit of the boys at Newport and did not insist on having his own measure taken up."[31]

It took Green some years to bring a Veterans Administration hospital to Rhode Island. He and Representative Forand tried unsuccessfully to introduce companion bills in 1937 authorizing one, but the Veterans Administration opposed the measure on the ground that Rhode Island veterans were receiving adequate treatment at the Newport Naval Hospital. However, many Rhode Islanders were hospitalized at Togus, Maine, forcing their relatives to travel hundreds of miles to visit them. Although Green badgered Frank Hines, the Veterans Administration administrator, to help support authorization for a hospital in Rhode Island, in 1940 Hines informed Green that a new hospital would be established in Massachusetts at West Roxbury, a location convenient to Rhode Island. And when that facility was completed in 1943, Hines argued that no consideration could be given to constructing an additional hospital in Rhode Island, in spite of an offer of state land for the site.[32]

In February 1944, after a talk at the White House with Green, Roosevelt sent a handwritten note to Hines urging him to give the matter his attention. In the following month Hines promised to give Rhode Island priority in future plans, and that summer the Federal Board of Hospitalization recommended that a hospital be built in Rhode Island. Hines met with Green at his home in Providence in November 1944 and visited several possible sites. When Green pressed the new administrator, General Omar Bradley, for action the following year, Bradley pointed out that the hospital was a huge undertaking and that Rhode Island would have its own facility in due course. Eventually Providence donated Davis Park, a forty-acre tract of land, and shortly after Roosevelt's death President Truman gave the project his approval. After inevitable slowdowns and bureaucratic errors, the four-hundred bed, seven-story structure was completed in 1948 at a cost of $5 million. Higgins made certain that wherever possible only Rhode Islanders were employed and that the manager of the hospital, Dr. William J. Sullivan, kept in close touch with Green's office. Patronage was the rule even to the landscaping of the grounds.[33]

Obviously, many of Green's opportunities for patronage resulted from his consistently strong support of Presidents Roosevelt and Truman, not only in the Senate but also during elections. Although he was not up for re-election in 1940, Green probably campaigned harder that year than in any other contest during his Senate career. Roosevelt's political popularity was at a low ebb in Rhode Island, and J. Howard McGrath was running for governor of the state against incumbent William Vanderbilt. The Democratic party, which had done poorly in the 1938 elections, hoped to recapture the major offices as well as the General Assembly; Green was also looking ahead to his own 1942 bid to retain his seat, when Republican Governor Vanderbilt would be a possible opponent. If McGrath won the governorship, Vanderbilt's chances of beating Green would be substantially reduced; and if Roosevelt fared well in Rhode Island in his bid for a third term and the Democrats carried many of the local elections, Green's position would be strengthened. These factors made 1940 a very important year for the seventy-three-year-old senator.

Opposition to Roosevelt stemmed from a variety of causes, all of which were involved in the third-term issue. Disenchantment with the New Deal, the persistence of depression conditions throughout the nation, and concern with Roosevelt's increasingly interventionist approach to European problems all reinforced opposition to a third term. In Rhode Island Roosevelt had won by a smaller margin in 1936 than in 1932, partly because several thousand Rhode Island Democrats, influenced by Father Coughlin, defected to the Union party candidate, William

Lemke. In March 1940 the Rhode Island legislature adopted a resolution requesting Congress to enact legislation preventing any president from seeking a third term. Copies of the resolution were transmitted to the state's congressional delegation, and Senator Gerry, always eager to thwart Roosevelt, introduced it in the Senate. Senator Green challenged the significance of the resolution, which, he pointed out, had passed the Rhode Island General Assembly by a bare majority. Moreover, while it advocated passage of legislation to prevent a president "from seeking a third term," it said nothing about the people or the Electoral College "electing a President for a third term, or about the possibility of Congress making a President ineligible for a third term."[34]

During the 1940 Democratic convention, Green, the national committeeman from Rhode Island, chaired a subcommittee that heard testimony on the merits of increasing the delegations of states in which the Democrats had won in the previous presidential election. Before 1936, when the two-thirds rule was abolished and rule by majority substituted, the southerners had been able virtually to veto nominations, and in 1940 they wanted a reward for their solid support of Roosevelt. Green proposed giving one additional delegate-at-large and one additional alternate to each state that had voted Democratic in 1936. Since this would have meant a bonus of one delegate to all but two of the states, the southerners countered with a proposal designed to regain for the South some of the influence it had lost in 1936: an additional three delegates for each state carried by the Democratic presidential candidate and an additional delegate for each congressional district that had either elected a Democratic representative or had cast at least fifteen thousand votes for its Democratic candidate for Congress. When this proposal was defeated by a voice vote, Green called for reduction of the number of delegates from Puerto Rico, the Virgin Islands, the Philippines, Alaska, Hawaii, and the District of Columbia—but not of those from the Canal Zone, one of whose delegates was Edward Higgins. Except for a suggestion that the delegations from doubtful states be enlarged, which was defeated by the subcommittee, the Democratic National Committee consented to the Green plan for apportioning delegates, and it was approved on the floor in the closing hours of the 1940 convention.[35]

After the nominations were settled, Green began to campaign, urging the rejection of "untried utility lawyer" Wendell Willkie. The American people, Green declared, ought not to be "frightened by the bogey of a third term" but should re-elect the man who had stood by them and "fought their battle" in the humiliating days of the depression; Roosevelt, he said, was willing to assume the responsibilities of a third term "not for further personal glory or a more exalted or secure place in history . . . but solely for his country's welfare" and, as the man best qualified by experience and training, should be returned to office.[36] On an eastern campaign trip Green praised Roosevelt's preparedness program and attacked the Republicans for disastrous shortsightedness in their attempts to block increased appropriations for ship and airplane construction, appropriations that "had to be used in the first place to make good all the omissions of preceding [Republican] administrations."[37] In a major radio address Green reviewed all the advantages that the New Deal and the social security system had brought to Rhode Island in the face of Republican opposition. He defended the president against the charge of President Henry M. Wriston of Brown University that a third term would be a serious blow to liberty, leading to tyrannical control by the executive over the Congress and the courts.[38]

The 1940 campaign for McGrath against Governor Vanderbilt proceeded along quite different lines. Green and Higgins seized the opportunity not only to aid their colleague but to discredit both the incumbent governor and the Republican party in Rhode Island by charging that Vanderbilt, in an effort to rid Pawtucket of a strong Democratic machine, had encouraged the use of wiretaps on the telephones of the organization's boss as well as on those of his own attorney general. Rhode Island had no law prohibiting wiretapping, but through the efforts of Green and McGrath, a select subcommittee of the Committee on Interstate Commerce began an investigation in May 1940, in the course of which Vanderbilt admitted that he had been responsible for hiring the organization that had done the tapping.[39] McGrath, who during the gubernatorial campaign accused Vanderbilt of being a henchman of blackmailers and wiretappers, soundly trounced him. Vanderbilt's defeat eliminated him as a possible candidate for Green's Senate seat and ended his political career.

In 1940 Roosevelt carried Rhode Island by an even greater margin than he had in 1932. Both House seats were won by Democrats, and Gerry was re-elected to the Senate. Although Green campaigned vigorously for Roosevelt and McGrath, he almost ignored Gerry's candidacy. Roosevelt ran ten thousand votes ahead of Gerry. Although the Republicans maintained their control of the state senate, Democrats won the four principal state offices as well as the lower house.

There had never been any doubt in Green's mind that he would seek a second term as United States senator in 1942. In campaigning in 1940 he had made much of his close friendship with the president, which he claimed had resulted in federal preference for Rhode Island. Irritated by the constant sounding of this political leitmotiv, the *Providence Journal* rebuked Green for using the theme to enhance his own prospects for re-election.[40] In 1942 Green delayed announcing his candidacy for nomination until two days before the Democratic state convention, but at the convention—after Eugene Sullivan, the representative from Green's home district, had praised him for standing "shoulder-to-shoulder with Roosevelt in the fight for the rights of man over the rights of property"—Green was nominated by acclamation.[41]

Ira Lloyd Letts, a former federal judge, was named by the Republicans to oppose Green in 1942. The campaign was one of the dullest in Rhode Island political history. In that first year of American participation in World War II, the electorate was more interested in national unity than partisan politics; news of American disasters and defeats in the Pacific and of an occasional victory crowded political news from the pages of the country's newspapers. Letts promised that if elected, he would provide wisely for the postwar period rather than let it be planned by "dreamers with Utopian disregard of preserving . . . the American standard of life,"[42] but neither he nor the rest of the Republican ticket ran a strong campaign.

Green spent most of the campaign period in Washington, carrying out his official business; he confined his campaigning to attending a few teas and giving one or two major addresses. In late October he told a partisan Rhode Island audience that he wanted to be returned to the Senate so that he could continue to play a part in the enactment of federal legislation of the kind that had been enacted on the state level in Rhode Island during his administration as governor. To the charge that he was nothing but a yes man to the president, Green replied, "One is not a follower when he goes before." Green offered no apologies "for upholding the hand of the President," for, he said, his constituents had sent him to Washington pledged to do just that; if they re-elected him he would continue to do so.[43]

A light vote was cast in November, and except for the state senate, the Democratic ticket swept to victory with heavy pluralities. Green received 58 per cent of the vote, an increase of 10 per cent over his vote in the 1936 election.[44]

In 1944 Green campaigned harder for Roosevelt's re-election than he had for his own in 1942, making numerous radio addresses in Rhode Island during late October and early November. The theme of all his speeches was that America could not afford to take a chance with a novice like Dewey who had refused to disavow the isolationist impulse of the Republican party. Winning the war was the paramount issue, according to Green, and the country could not do so without Roosevelt's leadership. Dewey was beaten decisively in Rhode Island as well as in the nation at large.[45]

In 1946 Gerry announced his retirement from the Senate, and McGrath immediately moved into contention for the seat. Despite the Republican sweep in the nation, the Democrats in Rhode Island fared well in 1946, among them McGrath. A shrewd politician who was at home in national Democratic circles, he quickly impressed the party's leadership, and within a year after his election to the Senate he was made chairman of the Democratic National Committee. McGrath's new prominence in the party was clearly beneficial to Green in the 1948 election year.[46]

In May 1947 former Representative Carroll Reece, chairman of the Republican National Committee, addressed a Republican audience in Rhode Island.[47] A week later Green in effect began his campaign for re-election by attacking Reece, the Republican party in general, and the Taft-Hartley bill in particular. He reveled in painting the Republicans as the party of doom, the privileged classes, and reaction. Anticipating Truman's later attack on the Eightieth Congress, he charged that it had crippled every government agency trying to protect the underprivileged and economically deprived from exploitation. He further termed the Republican-controlled Congress one of "undoing" rather than of "doing."[48] On Labor Day Green spoke of his liberal, prolabor record in the Senate and vehemently attacked the Taft-Hartley Act. When Taft made a precampaign speech in Rhode Island criticizing the New Deal, the Democratic party, and liberalism, Green countered by castigating Taft for his conservative leadership of the Senate Republicans. Green, at the age of eighty, once again took his place as a New Deal champion of the lower and middle classes, a staunch advocate of labor, and an internationalist; he spoke at meetings of labor unions, veterans' groups, and every conceivable ethnic minority within the narrow borders of the state. Labor unions quickly gave Green their support, and Higgins was confident that nothing could interfere with the senator's re-election.[49]

During the spring of 1948, Green was one of only three Democratic senators seeking re-election who supported Truman for the presidential nomination. Because of his loyalty to the president and his friendship with Democratic National Chairman McGrath, the senator from Rhode Island was appointed to the platform committee of the party at the national convention. He was also a member of the drafting committee that actually wrote the controversial 1948 Democratic platform. Truman's call for an extraordinary session of Congress after the conventions was applauded by Green, who was certain that it would prove that the Republicans in Congress would not fulfill the promises of their own platform, even when provided with an opportunity to do so before the campaign.

The Rhode Island Republican senatorial nominee was Thomas P. Hazard, a wealthy Rhode Islander who had been general treasurer of the state during the Vanderbilt administration. Although Hazard offered no effective opposition, Green engaged in a dynamic campaign in September and October to offset criticism of his advanced age. He went even further than Truman in his denunciation of the Republican Eightieth Congress. He vigorously attacked the House Un-American Activities Committee, which he criticized for conducting its investigations in "a way calculated to give the greatest publicity to the *investigators.*"[50] He pointed out that the choice facing the nation was between progress, as exemplified by the Democrats, and reaction, as manifested by the policies of the Republican party in the Eightieth Congress. Again and again he drew attention to his liberal voting record during his twelve years in office and promised to continue to work for expanded social security coverage, an increased minimum wage scale, adequate housing, price control, and a wise foreign policy. When the election returns were in, Green had defeated Hazard by almost sixty thousand votes.

In 1954, as in 1948, although others might have wondered whether he would run again, Green himself had no doubts. Because of the seniority he now had in the Senate, he was in line for the chairmanship of the Foreign Relations Committee. In spite of his advanced age, Green could not be denied renomination, for he was a popular figure in Rhode Island, his role in the Senate was a credit to the little state, and his financial contributions to the state Democratic party, quietly given and rarely publicized, were considerable. Green was a frugal millionaire who, through his aide and campaign manager, Higgins, donated carefully where it would do the most strategic good. His own campaigns for the Senate, furthermore, were paid for by himself, and what few donations he received were always passed on to the party. Governor Dennis J. Roberts made some attempts to obtain party support for himself, but the nomination went to Green, who embarked on another energetic campaign.[51]

As in 1948, he based his campaign on the iniquity of a Republican-controlled Congress. Green was best at attack, ridiculing the opposition, deriding the Republican party, and demonstrating to his constituents vitality, vigor, and political exuberance. Green delighted a Cranston audience on Indian Day by donning the headdress he was entitled to wear as an honorary chief sachem of the National Algonquin Indian Council and referring to himself as White Buffalo, his Indian name. At a Providence meeting of the executive committee of the Young Democratic Clubs of America he spoke as elder statesman and Foreign Relations Committee member, stressing the need for a bipartisan foreign policy. His Republican opponent, a lawyer named Walter Sundlun, was a lackluster candidate, whose campaign was half-hearted at best. Everett Dirksen as Republican senatorial campaign chairman spoke for Sundlun in Providence but carefully avoided attacking Green; very friendly relations existed between the Washington offices of the two senators.[52]

On 31 August 1954, during the campaign, Hurricane Carol lashed Rhode Island, causing over $200 million worth of damage, sixteen deaths, and many injuries. Downtown Providence was inundated by tidal waters, and the state's extensive coastline was devastated. Little warning of the hurricane's imminence having been given by the United States Weather Bureau, Green called an elaborately planned conference at his Washington office on 22 September to discuss the problems involved in obtaining accurate predictions of hurricane patterns and the lack of adequate warning facilities. Among those present were the acting chief of the Weather Bureau; weather specialists and forecasters; and weather officers of the navy, Coast Guard, Department of Commerce, and Civil Defense Administration. When Green criticized the federal agencies for failure to co-ordinate weather information or use it effectively, their representatives were able to convince him that the fault lay with Congress, which had not appropriated enough money to establish a reliable system of weather analysis and forecasting. So successful were they in interesting Green in the problems of the Weather Bureau that during the next few years he was largely responsible for appropriations of funds for hurricane analysis, hurricane watches, and improved forecasting facilities along the East Coast. The Army Corps of Engineers was therefore able to expedite hurricane studies and plans for hurricane barriers in coastal ports; and obsolete observation equipment, particularly that used in storm detection and tracking, was scrapped, and new equipment installed. Green and Senator Pastore successfully cosponsored several bills to improve Weather Bureau service.[53]

In the 1954 election Green received 59.3 per cent of the vote; sixty-one thousand more ballots were cast for him than for his opponent.[54] The publicity from his 22 September 1954 conference and his announcement that he would work to strengthen the Weather Bureau had given him an insurmountable advantage over Sundlun. Not only was Green's position bolstered as a senator whose seniority enabled him to influence federal agencies and summon government officials to his office; he was also able to play on the theme of Republican culpability (because half a million dollars had been eliminated from the Weather Bureau's budget request) for the devastation in Rhode Island that sufficient warning of Hurricane Carol's approach might have prevented. Moreover, Green had pounded away during the campaign at the Eighty-third Congress as antilabor and, as usual, had had the backing of organized labor in Rhode Island.[55] Finally, although the issue of his age had been raised during the campaign, Green had successfully dismissed it by replying that the question was not whether he was too old in 1954 but whether he would be too old when he ran for a sixth term at the age of ninety-nine.

Although he had ardently supported Roosevelt and Truman, Green devoted far less effort to the 1952 and 1956 campaigns of Adlai Stevenson, whom he considered indecisive. He campaigned lukewarmly for the Democratic national ticket in the 1952 election, in which Eisenhower took Rhode Island by a slim margin. By 1956 it was obvious that Eisenhower would be re-elected, and the Rhode Island Democratic organization conducted its electioneering as though the national campaign barely existed. Realizing that the state would not go Democratic in the presidential race and preferring not to jeopardize his amicable relationship with Eisenhower—especially since the chairmanship of the Foreign Relations Committee was in the offing—Green separated himself as much as possible from the national campaign.[56]

Perhaps more successfully than the majority of his fellow senators, Green managed to combine the seemingly incompatible demands of political life. He could and did play the statesman—

especially in the international sphere, as we shall see—and he had his modest successes as a legislator; he also fought vigorously for Rhode Island's interests. All of these roles seemed to come easily to him, as did the unexpectedly congenial role of politician. Green, the patrician and scholar, powerfully assisted by the indispensable Edward Higgins, not only performed the essential political chores but also played the role of politician with apparent relish. He enjoyed campaigning—the more bitterly partisan the better. Although Higgins took much of the initiative in patronage, Green participated actively. State politics continued to be a chief concern for him, for he remained convinced throughout his Washington years that he should not abdicate his responsibility to help guide the party at home. In short, Green was the rare senator who found no conflict in the roles of statesman-legislator and politician, and who actually enjoyed the roles equally.

6. Senate Leader

ANY institution—political, fraternal, or social—makes demands on its members beyond mere support of its objectives, but few institutions assume such importance to their members or exact such total loyalty as the United States Senate. Besides filling a representative and legislative role, a senator must play a series of subtle and interrelated roles within the Senate itself.

Foremost among these is the senator's relationship to the formal structure of the Senate: its committee system and its party leadership apparatus. Highly significant as a means of protecting or advancing home-state interests, committee memberships and seniority are even more important in terms of a career. The senator who hopes to attain influence within the Senate or the government can do so most readily through the committee structure.

Closely linked with exploitation of the committee system is the development by each senator of his own expertise in some policy area. Ideally the freshman chooses a specialty that is linked with his constituents' interests, that reflects his own personal tastes or concerns, and that relates to his early committee assignments. Then good luck and political longevity may win him a key chairmanship and a reputation as the leading expert or chief policy maker in that area.

More subtle is the fledgling senator's relation to his party's leadership in the Senate. One aspect of this is his loyalty to the party position on roll calls. Such loyalty is cherished by party leaders, and if a senator earns the special gratitude of his leader, so much the better, since a party leader not only needs the support of his party members, but has the capacity to reward it. These informal relationships are obviously not limited to senatorial ties with party leaders. Any political institution exhibits a complex pattern of interpersonal relations based as much on favors exchanged or expected as on friendship and philosophical compatibility.

Journalist William S. White and political scientist Donald Matthews have both concluded that there is an "establishment" or "inner club" in the Senate that rests ultimately on these informal patterns.[1] This central group is composed of the natural leaders—the influential and the senior members—and, above all, of those who most wholeheartedly accept Senate folkways and who single-mindedly identify themselves with the Senate as an institution. Inner club membership means power and a major voice in the functioning of the Senate. Not all freshmen seek status in the establishment and not all who do, win it. In some fashion, however, a freshman must work out his relationship to this informal network as well as to the formal patterns of power.

Along with all the other legislative issues on which he will be expected to take a stand during his first term, a freshman senator is certain to be confronted with some policy questions that are unique to the Senate. Constitutionally the Senate bears special responsibility for foreign affairs; in addition, sectional politics and Senate tradition have long given it a key role in civil rights discussions. Like all legislative bodies, occasionally it must also face vexing questions posed by the conduct of its own members. All of these matters, in one form or another, arose during the twenty-four years that Theodore Francis Green served in the Senate.

The first committee assignments the sixty-nine-year-old senator received after taking his seat in 1937 were to Appropriations, Post Offices and Post Roads, Privileges and Elections, and Public Buildings and Grounds. At that time, before the consolidation of major committees had been effected by the reform legislation of 1946, one major committee assignment and several minor ones (the latter often accepted reluctantly) were not uncommon. Foreign affairs had always been Green's primary interest, and he must have welcomed the opportunity in 1938 to drop the Post Office assignment to fill a vacant slot on the Foreign Relations Committee.[2] Although no evidence has survived to reveal how this shift was brought about, it is probable that both Majority Leader Alben Barkley and President Roosevelt were involved in it.

Green's committee responsibilities remained the same from 1938 until 1946: Foreign Relations, Appropriations, Privileges and Elections, and Public Buildings and Grounds. When the Republican-controlled Eightieth Congress was convened in January 1947, he was forced to exchange Foreign Relations for Rules; in 1949, however, with the resumption of Democratic control of the Senate, Green returned to his favorite committee assignment. In the reshuffling and consolidation that followed the 1946 reform legislation, he had to drop Appropriations, but from 1949 until he left the Senate in 1960, his assignments were Foreign Relations and Rules.

Green was very fortunate in being able to reconcile his intellectual interests, his desire for specialization, and the Senate committee system. He managed early in his career to have himself assigned to Foreign Relations, one of the choicest and most sought-after of committees. He served on that body for twenty of the twenty-four years he spent in Washington, his service interrupted for only two years and rewarded toward the end by the chairmanship. He was also fortunate that pressures from Rhode Island did not force him to seek a committee career in an area of intense concern to his state. He was thus free to indulge his long-standing interest in foreign affairs, which was fostered by the cosmopolitan tastes of a Yankee aristocrat, among them a love of world travel.

Green's relationship to the other major element of the formal structure of the Senate, the party leadership, was strengthened by adherence to the party position and the wishes of Democratic presidents. As long as the president and the Senate leadership concurred, his support could invariably be counted on by his floor leader. He could also be depended upon never to side with southern Democrats and Republicans against the northern liberal wing of his party. His consistent posture gave him high standing among his party peers.

His position in the Democratic hierarchy was further consolidated when Lyndon B. Johnson assumed party leadership. Johnson had become majority whip in 1951 after the electoral defeat of Scott Lucas of Illinois, the majority leader, and Francis Myers of Pennsylvania, the previous whip. Ernest McFarland of Arizona was chosen to succeed Lucas, and Johnson to succeed Myers. Although relations between Johnson and Green were not particularly close until the Texan became a floor leader, the Rhode Islander's dealings with Johnson's office had been carefully nurtured by Green's administrative assistant, Edward J. Higgins.

When the Republicans gained control of the Senate two years after Johnson's selection as whip and McFarland's as leader, the latter was defeated, leaving the Democratic floor leadership post again vacant. A party often elevates the man next in line to a vacant leadership post, but in this instance the fact that Johnson had been whip for so short a time cast some doubt on his candidacy. Furthermore, although he had been a staunch New Dealer, Johnson was now considered too conservative by the northern Democratic liberals. For the Texan to advance his claim to the position, he badly needed the support of at least one member of this wing of the Senate Democrats. Green was the only easterner on the Senate Policy Committee; while the Policy Committee had never been of paramount importance, membership on it still conferred some prestige.

Green faced a difficult choice when another candidate for the Democratic leadership—Senator James Murray of Montana, a staunch liberal with whom the Rhode Islander often agreed—sought his support. But the Johnson camp was active and well organized, and a telephone call from Senator Earle Clements just after the results of the November 1952 election became known prompted Green to give serious thought to the Texan's merit as potential leader. Although he and Johnson had not been close friends, Green not only respected Johnson's New Deal credentials but also believed that Johnson, being nearer to the center of the party spectrum, might lead the Senate Democrats (temporarily the minority party again) more effectively than Murray. He feared that a thoroughgoing liberal like the senator from Montana might divide the Democrats even more than they already had been in the aftermath of the sweeping Republican victory. Nevertheless, Green did not give Clements a firm answer.[3]

Higgins, who had worked closely with Johnson's office—and presumably with Johnson himself—viewed the party whip as the best candidate because of the benefits that might ultimately accrue to the Rhode Island senator. He therefore suggested to Clements that Johnson himself telephone Green to discuss his candidacy. After that call Green issued a public statement in support of Johnson; on his own initiative he also urged Murray to withdraw from the fight for the leadership on the grounds that Johnson was bound to win.[4]

The day before the Senate Democrats convened to make their choice, Johnson came to Green's office with the Senate patriarch, Richard Russell of Georgia, whose mastery of military policy as the leading Democrat on the Armed Services Committee Green had always admired. Russell was slated to make the speech nominating Johnson for the leadership; he and Johnson came to ask Green to make the seconding speech, so that Johnson's nomination would have the full weight of the Senate establishment in the person of Russell and the liberal northern credentials of Green. The next day, when the roll call was begun, to decide between Johnson and Murray, it soon became obvious that the latter was beaten, and he withdrew from the race.[5]

The support given by Green and Higgins to Johnson's successful candidacy undoubtedly worked to the advantage of the senator. From then on, the working relationship between the two senators—the one representing the nation's smallest state, the other its largest—became more intimate. Higgins's stature also grew proportionately, and he was quick to use his new strength on behalf of Green whenever an opportunity arose. In 1954 Johnson, with typical hyperbole but considerable sincerity as well, praised his Rhode Island colleague as one of "the towers of strength" of the Democratic party and an able senator whose friendship he cherished.[6] There is considerable evidence that his respect and affection were genuine. When he campaigned in Rhode Island in the fall of 1964, President Johnson made it a point to see his former colleague, who, in his ninety-seventh year, had been retired from the Senate for four years.

The civil rights issue has for years been of particular concern to the Senate, in which most of the twenty-two senators from the former Confederacy represent the last bastion of southern political power in the national government. The ease with which these southern senators have been able to accumulate seniority, their disproportionate influence in the inner club, and their use of the filibuster have made them a force to be reckoned with by proponents of any issue, like civil rights, in which the South has a strong interest.

Green consistently supported civil rights legislation during his Washington career. Although never an aggressive leader in the cause of the black man, Green lent it steady, though often passive, support, occasionally moving in from the periphery of a controversy to play a more active part.

In the late 1930s efforts to secure federal bans on the poll tax and on lynching were the chief civil rights activities. Early in his Senate career Green gave strong support to both. Indeed, in 1938, when the National Association for the Advancement of Colored People urged passage of a bill to make lynching a fed-

eral crime, Green's militant advocacy earned him southern re-
buke. A filibuster was mounted against the measure, and when
a motion was made to end the debate by imposing cloture
(which, according to Rule 22, required a two-thirds majority of
the total Senate), Green voted for cloture, but the move failed.[7]

The poll tax issue first came up during World War II; a bill
passed by the House in June 1943 was reported out favorably by
the Senate Judiciary Committee. In a radio interview Green
strongly advocated the legislation in the interests of raising national morale and showing "our allies in South America and Asia
that we are truly fighting for the democratic rights and privileges
contained in the Four Freedoms and the Atlantic Charter."[8]
Labor strongly backed the bill, which Green supported on the
floor of the Senate as well as on the air. Again the southerners
filibustered, and when the inevitable cloture attempt came, the
Rhode Islander voted for it. Only thirty-five other senators
shared his view, however, far short of the sixty-four necessary.
From 1938 to 1960 nine civil rights cloture votes were taken, and
all failed.[9] Efforts to pass fair employment practices legislation
met the same filibuster tactics and the same failure to impose
cloture.

Acute liberal frustration with this state of affairs led to a major
effort in 1947 to change Rule 22. A series of proposals to permit
smaller majorities to impose a halt to debate was made from both
sides of the aisle, but nothing was achieved. In 1951 still another
attack on the filibuster was mounted when Senators Green and
Pastore of Rhode Island joined nine other Democrats in sponsoring a resolution that would have reduced the two-thirds required to a simple majority. After hearings on this and other
proposals before the Senate Committee on Rules and Administration, of which Green was a member, it was voted to report out
a much milder revision, in which cloture would require the approval of two-thirds of those present and voting, not two-thirds
of the total membership. Green filed a separate minority report

with Senator William Benton, Democrat of Connecticut. Arguing that minority protection, the purported justification of the filibuster, had been turned into minority rule in the civil rights area, the two senators again proposed simple majority cloture and sought to apply it to motions to change the rules themselves.[10]

With this last recommendation Green and Benton raised one of the most intricate of the constitutional-parliamentary questions affecting the campaign against Rule 22. The southerners habitually filibustered motions made at the start of new Congresses to change the rules by which the Senate is governed. If the Senate were deemed a continuing body whose rules automatically carried over from the previous Congress, the two-thirds requirement of Rule 22 would carry over automatically and apply to that first reform motion. If the Senate were not a continuing body, however, it would begin each new Congress without any rules, would operate under normal parliamentary procedure, and could adopt or change rules by simple majority. The Democratic-controlled Senate of 1947 would not accept this approach, which Green favored; nor was the Republican-controlled Senate of 1953 more receptive when Green raised the same issue six years later.[11]

When the proposal was resubmitted in 1957, however, Vice-President Nixon, as president of the Senate, ruled that the Senate was not a continuing body and could adopt new rules at the opening of a new Congress. After extended debate Democratic Majority Leader Johnson persuaded his colleagues to table the motion to adopt new rules, 55 to 38, thus halting the effort to revise the cloture rule for that session. In his first break with the liberal record he had established on civil rights Senator Green voted with Johnson against use of the strategy he himself had strongly advocated in the past.[12] According to a memorandum filed with his papers, he believed that there were not yet enough votes to liberalize Rule 22 even if the way had been cleared to adopt new rules. He also wished to avoid Democratic division over the matter and hoped that a compromise could be worked out.[13] These reasons, however, were perhaps not as important as the relationship that had developed between Green and Johnson.

The following year, in the second session of the Eighty-fifth Congress, Green joined Democrat Thomas Hennings of Missouri and Republicans John Sherman Cooper of Kentucky, Jacob Javits of New York, and Clifford Case of New Jersey in supporting the kind of compromise that he apparently had hoped for earlier. It would have allowed cloture with the support of two-thirds of those present and voting (a plan he had condemned in a minority report seven years earlier) but added the proviso that if such a vote failed, another try could be made fifteen days later, at which time a majority of the Senate membership would suffice. The scheme made no headway in the 1958 session but gained partial acceptance the next year.[14]

At the opening of the first session of the Eighty-sixth Congress in 1959 a proposal for majority cloture sponsored by Democrat Paul Douglas of Illinois was defeated, 67 to 28. Thruston Morton of Kentucky, a moderate Republican, then proposed that three-fifths of those present and voting prevail for cloture, but this too went down to defeat, 58 to 36. Both times Green voted for reform. Ultimately Majority Leader Johnson produced a compromise that consisted of the first part of the Green-Hennings-Cooper-Javits-Case resolution of the year before: cloture to be invoked by two-thirds of those present and voting. When he brought it to a vote, 72 senators, including the Rhode Islander, were in favor and 22 against. The opposition was a mixture of liberals like Javits and Morse, who wanted to go further, and southern conservatives, who did not want to go nearly that far.[15] The moderating effect of Johnson's influence on Green was clearly evident in this instance.

During the fight two years earlier over the Civil Rights Act of

1957, another politically difficult and intricate issue arose over the question of whether jury trials should be guaranteed to persons cited for contempt of court for violating the voting rights of citizens. Liberals would normally have stood solidly behind such a right as trial by jury, but in this instance they were certain that southern juries would never convict those who barred Negroes from voting. Green and other liberals therefore felt impelled to vote against the southern amendment guaranteeing the jury trial.[16] Aware of the complicated cross-pressures at work and of the need for some kind of jury guarantee if any bill at all were to be passed, Johnson produced a typical compromise: jury trials were to be mandatory in cases of criminal, but not civil, contempt. The Senate spent many hours attempting to determine the distinction between the two.[17]

For the eastern liberal support he needed to get this proposal through, Johnson turned to Green. He not only sent Dean Acheson, whom he knew Green admired, to intercede for the compromise, but also used his own considerable powers of persuasion to convince the Rhode Island senator that without the compromise there would indeed be no bill at all and that adoption of the Johnson proposal would ensure passage of a fairly effective civil rights measure. The amendment was finally accepted, 51 to 42, and the whole bill passed, 72 to 18. Johnson thanked his stalwart supporter in a letter to which Green replied with praise for the majority leader's skill in unifying the Democrats behind this crucial measure.[18]

To conclude that Green bargained away his principles under pressure from Johnson would be to oversimplify a subtle relationship. In 1950 Green, now senior Senator from Rhode Island, maintained the same deep-seated convictions on civil rights that he had held upon his arrival in Washington. However, he had also chosen for himself the role of staunch partisan. Initially this had meant down-the-line support of Roosevelt and his New Deal, but after the simultaneous election of Eisenhower and elevation of Johnson to Democratic party leadership, Green supported his party chief in the Senate first, the president second. Furthermore, by the 1950s Green had become an influential member of the Senate inner club. Thus his policy position represented a blend of influences: his convictions, his party loyalty, his support of an admired leader (in some degree Green may have regarded Johnson as the inheritor of Roosevelt's mantle), and his position as a respected elder of the Senate. Green was a Senate man, with all that that implied.

The issue that most severely tried the Senate as an institution during Green's tenure grew out of the strident, often vicious anti-Communism of the late 1940s and early 1950s. The trend was most blatantly exploited by Senator Joseph R. McCarthy, but concern with the internal Communist menace began manifesting itself on Capitol Hill some time before the Wisconsin senator discovered its political potential. There was, for instance, the unenlightened immigration legislation passed by the Republican Eightieth Congress in June 1948 and reluctantly signed by President Truman. Green, who came from a state in which many inhabitants were descendants of relatively recent immigrants, had hoped that some of the liberalizing proposals would survive.[19]

In 1952 the Rhode Island senator voted against the McCarran-Walter bill on immigration because of its restrictive provisions; he later voted with the minority to uphold Truman's veto.[20] Subsequently, although with little success, he also joined other senators in sponsoring liberalizing legislation. In doing so he acted on his own convictions as well as in response to pressures from ethnic groups in his state. Almost the only concession that could be wrung from a reluctant Congress in that period of insecurity, however, was the admission in 1956 of Hungarian refugees from Communist repression.

Closer to the heart of the anti-Communist controversy were

various legislative schemes for insuring the nation's internal security. Unlike Senator Patrick McCarran, one of the leading crusaders for such legislation, Green was deeply offended by many of the measures proposed in Congress as well as by some of the procedures followed by its committees. He was never tempted to take political advantage of the anti-Communist hysteria sweeping the country, even though he represented a predominantly Catholic state in which many voters, even before the Spanish Civil War, had been taught to hate Communism as inimical to their faith.

In 1950 Congress passed the McCarran Act on internal security over President Truman's veto. Green, who abhorred the potential violations of civil liberties that its provisions permitted, was applauded by the American Civil Liberties Union for endorsing the Truman veto. When the Rhode Island department of the American Legion urged him to cast his vote to override the president, Green expressed pride in having been one of the seven senators who had opposed the bill as detrimental to civil liberties and rights.[21]

For Senator McCarthy, Green reserved a special measure of disdain. Until 9 February 1950, when McCarthy delivered his famous Lincoln Day speech in Wheeling, West Virginia, in which he claimed to know the precise number of Communists still active in the State Department, he had been known for little more than his relatively industrious support of the economic interests of his state, especially the fur industry. The Wheeling speech revealed to him the extent of the political mileage to be gained by attacking Communism in government; it also marked the beginning of a growing involvement by the Senate in the issue and in the antics of its foremost exploiter.

Senator Green was not a member of the committee that finally brought McCarthy to book and censured him, but he was deeply involved in an earlier investigation of the Wisconsinite. It was not clear whether in his Wheeling speech McCarthy had claimed that there were 57, 81, or 205 Communists in the State Department.[22] An ensuing rash of charges and countercharges on the Senate floor prompted the Democratic leadership to authorize a Foreign Relations Committee investigation of the McCarthy allegations involving the State Department, and a special subcommittee was appointed. Chaired by Millard Tydings of Maryland, it included two other Democrats, Green and Brian McMahon of Connecticut, and two Republicans, Bourke Hickenlooper of Iowa and Henry Cabot Lodge of Massachusetts.[23] Hickenlooper was the only member of the subcommittee with any sympathy for either McCarthy or his activities. The three Democrats were liberals and administration supporters, committed to the Roosevelt-Truman record, and Lodge, though a Republican, was certainly from the more liberal wing of the party. Thus, the majority of the subcommittee, in addition to the difficulties of the investigation itself, faced the ticklish problem of avoiding attack for bias from the pro-McCarthy press. It was an unenviable assignment at best.

The investigation itself was impeded at every turn by the tactics and personality of the subcommittee's star witness. Rather than presenting whatever evidence he might have had to substantiate his charges, McCarthy was evasive. In all probability this reluctance to co-operate reflected the fact that he had very little evidence to lay before his colleagues. Early in the hearings Green asked if McCarthy could support his charge that Professor Owen Lattimore of The Johns Hopkins University was the top Soviet espionage agent in the United States or if this sweeping accusation was merely suspicion. McCarthy replied, as he would throughout the hearings, that files kept by the Federal Bureau of Investigation would bear him out. Green and his subcommittee associates vainly urged McCarthy to substantiate his assertions. Eventually, the Wisconsin senator admitted that he had not seen any FBI files himself.[24]

Later in the hearings, when other witnesses appeared, Green's questioning revealed some of his personal reactions to the affair. When the distinguished ambassador and Columbia University professor, Philip Jessup, appeared, the Rhode Islander remarked that Jessup was fortunate to have highly-placed friends like George Marshall and Dwight Eisenhower to write character references for him to offset the McCarthy charges. "What would have happened to you [if] you were unknown instead of known?" he asked, for the permanent destruction of the reputations of younger State Department and especially Foreign Service personnel was the inevitable result of McCarthy's tactics. Green perceived clearly the "terrible effect on the success of our foreign policies" that this shattering of confidence in the State Department would bring about.[25]

The risks inherent in the role of investigator are well illustrated by an exchange between Green and Louis Budenz, the former top Communist party leader, who had recanted and joined the Communist hunters. The senator asked Budenz why he had not been called to testify during the lengthy 1949 trial of leading Communists in the New York federal court that had resulted in convictions for subversion under the Smith Act. But, as Budenz pointed out to his inquisitor, he had actually been the first witness in that trial on behalf of the government, and the pro-McCarthy press criticized Green for knowing little about the Communist menace and the threat it posed. One Hearst paper said that Green "was so anxious to trip Budenz, he kicked himself" and showed that he was "an ignorant if not a stupid man."[26]

As part of this same inquiry into charges about State Department personnel and procedures, Senator Lodge and Senator Green were sent to Europe as a special subcommittee to study State Department security procedures in major embassies. After conducting hearings in Frankfurt, Paris, New York, and Washington, and questioning thirty-four State Department employees, they concluded that in general security was good, but that procedures in Germany could be tightened.[27]

The Tydings subcommittee hearings were finally over in July 1950. In its report the three-man Democratic majority accused Senator McCarthy of knowingly misinterpreting the facts and termed his accusations "a fraud and a hoax perpetrated on the Senate of the United States and the American people."[28] Because the two Republicans could not associate themselves with such strong language about a fellow party member, they took refuge in a criticism of the procedures followed by the subcommittee. According to them, it should have made an independent examination of its own instead of trying to dispute the McCarthy charges.

The risks run by the Wisconsin senator's opponents on the subcommittee and elsewhere are dramatically illustrated by the defeat of Millard Tydings when he ran for re-election in 1950. McCarthy led the attack in Maryland, and unquestionably his involvement, plus the role Tydings had played as chief investigator, played a part in the outcome. The elections in 1952 that gave the Republicans brief control of Congress enabled McCarthy to broaden his attacks, as chairman of the Senate Government Operations Committee and its Subcommittee on Investigations. Ultimately, however, the threat that his wild charges and destructive tactics posed to the Senate led to his downfall. In fact, it was this threat, rather than disagreement with his objectives or tactics in themselves, that brought reluctant Senate action against him.

Finally, in 1954, another committee of the Senate was specially chosen to investigate the conduct of the Wisconsin senator, and in the same year it recommended that he be censured for conduct unbecoming a senator. Many of Green's constituents roundly condemned the report and demanded that he oppose censure on the floor. These pressures notwithstanding, when the vote came on 1 December 1954, Green cast his vote for censure.[29]

Unquestionably, Green's interest in foreign affairs was the center around which all else revolved in his Senate career. While he devoted himself wholeheartedly to all his senatorial roles, he immersed himself completely in the details of foreign policy. Not surprisingly, foreign relations became his acknowledged specialty within the Senate's informal division of labor, and he finally won the cherished power and prestige of the Foreign Relations Committee chairmanship.

Senator Green had proven himself a staunch internationalist both in prewar tilts with the isolationists and during struggles over the neutrality legislation. He had championed Roosevelt's prewar efforts to alert the nation to the dangers posed by aggressive totalitarianism, and, long convinced that American membership in the League of Nations could have averted World War II, Green actively supported the United Nations idea as the war drew to a close. His interest in international co-operation was allied with his abiding concern for social welfare at home, for he advocated careful planning at home and abroad after the war.[30]

By the end of the war the Rhode Islander had become well known among his Senate colleagues for his strong convictions on international co-operation. Throughout the Foreign Relations Committee hearings on the United Nations charter, there was never any question about his position. In a radio speech in July 1945 he called for every possible additional vote in the Senate above the two-thirds needed for ratification so that an overwhelming endorsement would give the world added proof that America "was at last assuming that world leadership to which she was entitled."[31] Green himself was active as the war neared its end in securing the establishment of the United Nations Relief and Rehabilitation Administration (UNRRA). The ramifications of this relatively noncontroversial effort, as they developed, were of far-reaching importance. The process began with State Department negotiations for an international arrangement, that was to take the form of an executive agreement, on the feeding and clothing of the people of war-ravaged countries. The Senate Foreign Relations Committee, however, upon learning of the plan, expressed the view that a formal treaty would be a more appropriate vehicle. Chairman Thomas Connally of Texas thereupon appointed a special subcommittee to investigate the problem. Its members were: Green; Elbert Thomas of Utah; Robert LaFollette, Jr., of Wisconsin; and Arthur Vandenberg of Michigan.[32]

Not forgotten, especially by Senator Green, were memories of 1919 and the disastrous result of the failure then to make provision for adequate Senate involvement in the peace settlement. Green and Vandenberg were assigned the task of conferring with the State Department on the actual form of the agreement. During a summer recess in the year-long 1943 session of Congress, Francis B. Sayre, special assistant to the secretary of state, came to Providence for a conference with Green at his home on John Street. They concluded that a purely executive agreement would not be desirable in light of the problems that soon would arise during the general postwar settlement, that a precedent of "close and vital co-operation between the legislative and executive branches" should be established.[33] The efforts of many others undoubtedly contributed to the co-operation that smoothed the negotiation and ratification of both the charter and the various treaties, but the importance of this early move cannot be discounted.

Eventually, a compromise was reached on UNRRA: Congress would enact general authorization for the agency and appropriate necessary funds; the president could then make individual agreements with other countries to set the machinery in motion.[34] Some senators believed that in the compromise the subcommittee had given up too much of its power, others that it had gained too little. It was also argued that without the binding force of a treaty, Congress might shirk a future obligation undertaken in this less formal way or that the Senate might be bypassed similarly in the future if the two-thirds vote needed to ratify a treaty could not be achieved. Green defended the compromise his subcommittee had sponsored.[35] Although publicly he argued that no binding precedent was involved, privately he hoped that a precedent had been set for bypassing two-thirds of the Senate with majorities in both houses, for he was convinced that the two-thirds rule was undemocratic.[36]

Green staunchly supported the White House during the revolution in American foreign policy that occurred in the late forties, as the nation, having shifted rapidly from isolationism to leadership of a vast wartime coalition, took up the unfamiliar role of peacetime leader of the free world. Radical as this new role may have seemed to many Americans—among them many senators—it merely confirmed convictions that the Rhode Islander had held since the Wilson era. These convictions, perhaps more than personal devotion to Truman, made him almost invariably a firm administration partisan on foreign policy questions.

In 1947, for example, Green supported the president when he announced the Truman Doctrine, which committed the United States to fill the gap left by British withdrawal from Greece and Turkey. He refuted criticisms of the president's stand both in public statements and in letters. Green also gave his full support to the North Atlantic Treaty and the organizational structure for which it provided. The president's decision to intervene in Korea when the North Koreans invaded South Korea met with Green's unqualified approval because the move was quickly placed under the jurisdiction of the United Nations; this made it a collective resistance to aggression rather than a unilateral American move. Moreover, Green argued, intervention by the United Nations was essential to its own survival as well as to that of the South Koreans: the failure of the League of Nations to act in similar circumstances had led to its demise.[37]

In general, the senator viewed with skepticism overseas actions taken by the United States independently of the world organization. In discussions on Southeast Asia policy with Secretary of State John Foster Dulles, Green expressed the fear that America might sometime be tempted to act unilaterally and that the result would cast this country in the role of a colonial power in the eyes of Asian anticolonial movements.[38] Later developments in Vietnam seem to have borne out his concern.

In recognition of Green's strong support of the United Nations, President Truman in September 1952 appointed him a member of the United States delegation to the Seventh General Assembly. The senator used this opportunity to reiterate his faith in the world organization and the approach to international problems that it represented. Insisting that the United Nations was the "last great hope of mankind," Green called for "unswerving determination until it shall become the great and compelling force its framers envisioned."[39] After the November election, on the assumption that the new president would want to appoint his own delegates, Green submitted his resignation, which, however, Eisenhower refused to accept.[40]

During the period following announcement of the Truman Doctrine and the implementation of the Marshall Plan, foreign aid became the policy area in which the need for steady year-in, year-out support was greatest. Senator Green had supported the establishment and the program of the Economic Co-operation Administration through which the Marshall Plan was implemented, and he stoutly defended the annual appropriations sought for the ECA, which were incessantly attacked by fiscal and foreign policy conservatives.[41]

Certain firm convictions about foreign aid not only placed Green in frequent opposition to his Senate colleagues but also caused him to raise occasional questions about the policies of the administration. For example, he felt very strongly that economic aid should be made available in such a way that it would directly benefit the common people in the nations concerned; he did not subscribe to the notion that money flowing first to the local elite would eventually trickle down to the masses. In 1950 he objected to the American aid program for Spain on the ground that it was a mistake to give funds to the Franco regime without adequate assurance that they would be used to benefit the Spanish people as a whole. In fact, in that year he even joined fourteen other senators in voting against a $100-million grant to Spain because it contained no such guarantee.[42]

In 1951 he led a bipartisan Foreign Relations Committee group to Europe to investigate the impact of American aid programs. Green was basically opposed to congressional junkets, and this was no pleasure trip: under the energetic Rhode Islander's direction the subcommittee conducted fourteen days of hearings in Paris, London, Madrid, Athens, Ankara, Rome, and Frankfurt. Green returned convinced, if he had not been before, that it was in our "enlightened self-interest" to help Western Europe, Greece, and Turkey, primarily with economic, as opposed to military, aid.[43]

The 1951 aid recommendations from the administration totaled $8.5 billion, of which only $2 billion was earmarked for economic aid, the rest having been allocated to military assistance of various kinds. When the bill reached the Senate, conservative Senators Harry Byrd and Robert Taft joined Foreign Relations Committee Chairman Connally in a move to cut economic aid in half. In spite of Green's vigorous efforts to prevent the slash, the bill went to the Senate floor reduced by $1 billion. During floor consideration the Rhode Islander offered an amendment in behalf of himself and Democratic Senators William Fulbright of Arkansas, Brian McMahon of Connecticut, and John Sparkman of Alabama. This effort failed, winning the support of only seventeen hard-core liberal internationalists.[44]

With the advent of the Eisenhower administration, the fears that economic aid would be further downgraded prompted a Senate delegation to make strong protests to the White House. Correspondence between Green and Harold Stassen, Eisenhower's director of the Foreign Operations Administration, and subsequent experience with the new administration's policies partially allayed those fears.[45] Continuing his active interest in foreign aid until his retirement from the Senate, Green in 1955 traveled extensively in Southeast Asia, the area to which the emphasis in aid had been shifting. On this and other trips he sought to analyze basic policy needs and to effect changes to meet them.

As president, Harry Truman presided over other major policy innovations besides that of foreign aid; in fact, the Missourian may be considered the architect of our Middle East policy. In this area, too, Green's longstanding beliefs assured his stout support. His concern for the Jews as a group was virtually a family legacy. His great-great-grandfather, Dr. John Green, had befriended one of the prominent Jewish families of Newport during the Revolution, when the British had occupied the city. During Green's career at the state level he saw the political allegiance of the fairly substantial Rhode Island Jewish community shift from Republican loyalty to support of FDR in recognition of his strong anti-Nazi stand.[46]

Apparently Rhode Island Jews saw in Green a staunch proponent of the religious tolerance he had inherited from his intellectual idol Roger Williams and therefore a potential spokesman for their cause. Not long after he became a senator, a delegation of Jewish leaders asked him to urge President Roosevelt to press the British to implement the Balfour Declaration. A Jewish national home in Palestine had become even more important than before to the Jews as a result of Nazi persecution. Green enthusiastically lent his support and made a strong appeal to the White House.[47]

During the prewar period, even in the face of some opposition from constituents, he supported Jewish aspirations and took every opportunity to help the victims of German persecution. In the spring of 1945 Green planned to introduce a resolution in the Senate—with Republicans Warren Austin of Vermont and Styles Bridges of New Hampshire as cosponsors—for the establishment of Palestine as a Jewish homeland. On 16 May, however, Under Secretary of State Joseph C. Grew asked him not to do so, lest his action upset British-American relations and openly conflict with State Department policy.[48] Green reluctantly agreed.

In September 1945, with the Rhode Island congressional delegates and other prominent Rhode Islanders, Green memorialized President Truman on the Palestine problem. Also that fall Green and Democrat Robert Wagner of New York, another strong advocate of a Jewish homeland in Palestine, prepared a second resolution, similar to the one Green had sponsored in May, and secured the cosponsorship of the Ohio Republican, Senator Robert Taft. Senator Connally of Texas, chairman of the Foreign Relations Committee, pressed by Green to back the move, appointed a subcommittee, with the Rhode Islander as chairman, to study the resolutions on the subject that had accumulated in the committee's files.[49] The subcommittee soon concluded that the time had come for the Congress to "give expression to its views on the need for the restoration of Palestine as the Jewish National Homeland" and offered a redrafted resolution to that effect. The resolution was accepted by the full Foreign Relations Committee, 17 to 1, with Connally the lone dissenter. It quickly passed the Senate without a record vote on 17 December and was accepted by the House two days later.[50] This resolution, to which Green had contributed so much, bore fruit in White House recognition of the new state of Israel in May 1948.

The foreign policy question that elicited the Rhode Islander's staunchest support for Truman was a product of the Korean imbroglio. In a dramatic, though hardly unexpected, move in April 1951 the commander-in-chief relieved General of the Army Douglas MacArthur of his Far Eastern commands because of his public opposition to the president's policy of limiting the war to the Korean peninsula.

MacArthur's dismissal, his subsequent triumphant return to the States, and his melodramatic address to a joint session of Congress produced a public furor. The Senate initiated an investigation into the facts of the dismissal; it was to be conducted jointly by the Armed Forces and the Foreign Relations Committees. Inevitably the hearings became a full-dress inquiry into such matters as Far Eastern policy and the issue of civilian control of the military. During the lengthy sessions, in which many witnesses were heard, Green played an active part in the questioning. On the very first day, as he interrogated MacArthur himself, one of the crucial themes Green was to pursue with later witnesses emerged: American co-operation with the United Nations versus pursuit of a unilateral policy. The general was forced to admit that he was prepared to continue his military policies alone if the United Nations withdrew its support from the United States. This, of course, was unacceptable to the senator.[51]

As the proceedings went on day after day, Green took his turn in questioning each successive witness. Besides the issue of United Nations support as opposed to a go-it-alone policy, he tried to show that MacArthur's policies would bring on a third world war, a nuclear holocaust.[52] The essence of the Rhode Islander's position is summed up in his interrogation of Major General David G. Barr: "We should be loath to spread war, not only because it might lead to the third world war, and not only because it would draw the Russians into it, but also because it is an immoral act, against the principles of the United Nations which we have helped to set up and which we regard as the principal hope for peace in the world. Is that not true?"[53]

Throughout this period of intense policy debate and political conflict, Green, though he did not play a major part, steadfastly supported Truman's foreign policy. In foreign relations as in domestic affairs, Green, with insignificant exceptions, backed the programs of presidents of his own party. He believed that the president was vested with primary responsibility for foreign affairs and that the Senate should support him except in rare instances when disagreement was inescapable.

Green's views on foreign policy are illustrated by his record during the Eisenhower administration. It is largely a record of co-operation, even though Green's seniority on the Foreign Relations Committee might have made him a formidable opponent to the Republican occupant of the White House. The tone of the period was set by the controversy over the so-called Bricker Amendment, a proposal fathered by Republican Senator John W. Bricker of Ohio and devised to limit the president's power to make foreign policy decisions on his own initiative, particularly through executive agreement. A bipartisan group of fifty-nine senators supported the proposal when it was brought to the floor in February 1952.[54]

Both President Truman and President Eisenhower opposed the amendment, although the latter was less adamant. Senator Green, who believed strongly that such a curb on the president's power to conduct foreign affairs should not be added to the Constitution, for once had the satisfaction of receiving support not only from such important Rhode Islanders as Zechariah Chafee, Jr., and Henry M. Wriston, the president of Brown University, but also from the *Providence Journal;* rarely did that newspaper and the senator agree.[55] When a Senate vote was taken on a substitute version of the Bricker proposal, it barely missed passage by the required two-thirds majority. The vote was 60 to 31, with Green among the thirty-one opponents.[56]

In 1957, Green, at the age of 89, became chairman of the Senate Committee on Foreign Relations. Thus, in the middle of Eisenhower's tenure, the senior Rhode Island senator had an eleventh-hour opportunity to put into practice his conception of the proper roles of the committee and the Senate in foreign affairs. In spite of his age, it would be unfair to label his assumption of the chairmanship a failure of the seniority system. Intellectually he was exceptionally well prepared for the position, and age as yet had undermined him neither mentally nor physically.

Although some of his Senate colleagues questioned his capacity to meet the strenuous demands of the chairmanship and others were disturbed by the image that his accession might convey to the rest of the world, no one challenged the seniority process. His meticulous attention to detail—though considered picayunish by one Republican on the committee—had earned him the solid respect of his peers.[57]

Majority Leader Johnson, the senior party official with whom Green would work closely, considered Green's wealth of experience invaluable and appreciated his ability to get things done "when others just talk and get headlines."[58] Foreign affairs were not the majority leader's special interest. During the tenures of Green's immediate predecessors—Alexander Wiley of Wisconsin, who served during the Republican Eighty-third Congress, and Walter George of Georgia, chairman for the next two years—Johnson had paid little attention to the work of the committee. Like Senator George, Johnson considered it his duty to support President Eisenhower whenever he could.

Senator Green also advocated a bipartisan foreign policy and generally supported the White House, but he kept his own counsel. Although the majority leader and the committee's staff found it difficult to determine what the chairman really thought, Green's approach to committee business was judicious and independent:

> There come before these committees, among others, experts
> for the Army, Navy, and State Departments who give us
> full information, much of it confidential. I have in each
> instance decided how I should vote. I have decided without
> regard to what effect my vote might have on my personal
> fortunes, and solely with regard to what I believe to be for
> the best interest of our country.[59]

As a result of Green's independence, Johnson's involvement with foreign policy, such as it was, was through the Eisenhower administration itself as often as through the committee chairman; the majority leader, however, frequently employed the professional committee staff and Green's assistant, Edward Higgins, as his channel of communication with Green.[60]

The views Green brought to the chairmanship concerning the proper function of the committee were clearly foreshadowed by his earlier attitudes: that the conduct of foreign affairs should be nonpartisan, that the primary responsibility for foreign affairs was the president's, although the Senate (not necessarily the committee alone) had the right to influence foreign policy through its legislative functions; and that the role of Congress was essentially educational. To fulfill the latter role, the committee under Green continued to sponsor in-depth studies of American foreign policy by private research groups. In none of his assumptions about his own or the committee's role did Green's views represent a major break with the recent past: both George and Wiley had run the committee along similarly noncontentious lines.

In both 1957 and 1958 the new chairman accepted the modifications that were introduced in foreign aid requests by the Eisenhower administration (which, having inherited its foreign aid policy, generally sought to continue it unchanged). In 1957, for example, assistance under the Mutual Security Program was for the first time to take the form of loans rather than grants. In that year the bill, contrary to usual practice, was introduced first in the Senate. Green piloted it through the committee and then acted as floor manager for it. In both years the amount finally appropriated, although cut in the House, was approximately that which the president had requested. Minority Leader William Knowland praised Green for his skill in steering the bills through the committee and for his fairness.[61]

Such harmony, however, did not always prevail. In 1957 President Eisenhower sent to the Senate the nomination of Scott McLeod for the post of American ambassador to Ireland. Because of McLeod's heavy-handed treatment of suspected Communists during his tenure as chief security officer of the Department of State, Democratic liberals opposed the nomination, as did the chairman of the Foreign Relations Committee. When the nomination came to a vote in that body, Green joined five others in a minority vote against McLeod, while nine committee members supported the president's choice. On the floor Green took a strong opposing stand. When the Senate finally voted, Green and the liberals lost, 54 to 22, and the nomination was approved. Democratic National Chairman Paul Butler praised Green for voting against McLeod.[62] Not all Irish-Americans agreed, however, and Green received many irate letters from his constituents.[63]

One of the most volatile issues that emerged during Green's period as chairman—and one that took much of his time throughout 1957—involved the Middle East. In early January 1957, just after Green had assumed the chairmanship of the Foreign Relations Committee, the general tenseness of the situation there prompted the president to request congressional authority to use American armed forces if necessary to preserve the independence of Middle Eastern countries against Communist aggression. In true bipartisan spirit, Green, acting for himself and Senator Wiley, his ranking minority counterpart on the committee, introduced such a resolution; in doing so he placed the support of the chairmanship behind the White House request even though some of his Democratic colleagues were disturbed by the wording of the proposal.

At joint hearings held by the Senate Armed Services and Foreign Relations Committees and chaired by Senator Green, a parade of administration witnesses headed by Secretary of State John Foster Dulles supported the resolution and testified to the urgency of the situation in the Middle East. A majority of the Democrats on the joint body, however, did not want to put Congress on record as specifically authorizing presidential use of troops. They preferred a simple "sense of Congress" assertion that peace in the area should be preserved. Four Democrats, including Green and Senator John F. Kennedy (a freshman, and recently admitted to the committee through the efforts of Green and Higgins), joined the Republicans in supporting the original version.[64]

Although this bipartisan group had a majority, it was evident that only a compromise rewording of the proposal would prevent serious trouble for the administration; accordingly, a new version was worked out that avoided direct authorization for the president by asserting that "the United States is prepared to use armed forces." Since the president as commander-in-chief had the power to order military forces to the area with or without congressional sanction, Green accepted the new wording. The revised resolution was voted out for floor action by the Republicans and some of the Democrats, among them Green, over the opposition of the remaining Democrats.[65]

The Foreign Relations Committee chairman, acting for the joint committee, reported the resolution to the Senate with his full support. While voicing his concern at partisan overtones in the committee consideration of the resolution, Green also insisted that the Senate was not and never would be a rubber stamp for the president's foreign policy. In March the Senate approved what would later be termed the Eisenhower Doctrine, 72 to 19. Green was satisfied with the result, and a year later, in April 1958, pronounced the doctrine a relative success.[66]

In May 1958 a crisis of the sort contemplated by the doctrine arose in Lebanon, whose government was being challenged with the support of the left-wing regime in Syria. The president decided that the United States would have to take action against the threat of Communist subversion in Lebanon and in July ordered troops into that country to take control of the strategic points. Between the troops' arrival and their departure in October, the problem was taken to the United Nations, where the Arab states agreed to stop fomenting internal dissension within each other's borders. Senator Green backed Eisenhower's action in sending troops and approved even more of his prompt referral of the problem to the United Nations. American intervention abroad, in Green's view, was justified only if endorsed by the world organization.[67]

A major departure from his customary support of presidential initiative in foreign policy was Senator Green's sharp disagreement with the Eisenhower administration over Quemoy and Matsu. The Formosa Resolution had been passed by Congress in 1955 as a result of constant bombardment in late 1954 of two small islands, garrisoned by Nationalist troops, off the coast of Red China. The president and the secretary of state wanted congressional confirmation of their view that America's commitment to defend Formosa under an earlier treaty also extended to the Pescadores Islands and, by implication, to Quemoy and Matsu.

Democrats Walter George of Georgia (then Foreign Relations Committee chairman), Richard Russell of Georgia, and Green, and Republicans William Knowland of California and Leverett Saltonstall of Massachusetts introduced Senate Joint Resolution 28 to implement the White House request. The Rhode Islander associated himself with this bipartisan endorsement of presidential policy because he believed that, having identified its interests with those of Nationalist China, the United States was obligated to defend Formosa. Green felt that the pledge to defend the offshore islands was only being made as part of the American commitment to defend Formosa, that it was not a blanket endorsement of any move the president might wish to make to check Communist expansion in the Far East.[68]

Congress passed the resolution quickly, with little opposition, and not until three years later, in the summer and fall of 1958, did the possibility of action under it become an issue. In August, while the United Nations was considering the Lebanon problem, intelligence reports of Communist activity that threatened the security of Quemoy and Matsu alarmed the administration. On

4 September the secretary of state asserted that the United States was prepared to defend the islands. A week later, in a televised address, President Eisenhower announced that he interpreted the Formosa Resolution as authorizing action by him "as circumstances dictated."[69]

Most members of Congress either reacted favorably to the position that the president had taken or acquiesced in the chief executive's view of the latitude permitted him by the resolution. The ninety-one-year-old chairman of the Senate Foreign Relations Committee was one of the few who disagreed. Green was convinced that the president's interpretation of his mandate was too broad. It seemed to Green that the White House was now seeking to justify intervention in Quemoy as a means of preventing a general spread of Red Chinese aggression rather than as a defense measure for Formosa. If the president was convinced that the threat posed by mainland China had taken on a new and wider dimension, the senator argued, he should turn to Congress for policy guidance.[70]

On 29 September Green wrote to President Eisenhower presenting his views in detail. He argued again that military action should not be taken by the president unless he was "sure beyond any reasonable doubt that the security of Formosa itself" was involved. He also raised the question of whether Quemoy was indeed essential to the defense of Formosa, two hundred miles away. "My decision to send this letter to you," he told the president, "has involved a great deal of soul-searching on my part. At one point I seriously contemplated calling the Committee on Foreign Relations back to Washington so that it might meet with cabinet members to learn fully the nature of our possible involvement."[71] He had rejected this course, he wrote, lest it upset the negotiations that were in progress, and there had not been time to poll the committee members. In the last sentence of the letter he noted that he was sending a copy to Majority Leader Johnson.

The president did not take lightly this unaccustomed opposition from the Senate's senior foreign policy expert. Since Congress had already adjourned, he sent a strongly argued defense of his view to Green, in which he insisted on the importance of events in the Formosa Strait to the security of the United States and the free world, and assured Green that "neither you nor any other American need feel that the United States will be involved in military hostilities merely in defense of Quemoy and Matsu."[72]

Disenchanted by now with Eisenhower's foreign policy, Green accused the administration of vacillation, of seeking alternately to avoid antagonizing the Communists and to avoid offending Chiang Kai-shek. "Never," he went on to say, "have we had the courage to say to the other countries of the world that the United Nations ought to be called into this situation."[73] Green's criticism prompted Senator H. Alexander Smith, New Jersey Republican and fellow member of the Foreign Relations Committee, to deny that the chairman spoke for his committee colleagues.[74] Green's new hostility to the president's foreign policy may have been caused by more than disagreement with Eisenhower's interpretation of the Formosa Resolution; Green may have felt slighted as chief Senate spokesman on foreign affairs because the president rarely consulted him.

One of the most controversial issues to arise in the televised debates between John Kennedy and Richard Nixon during the 1960 presidential campaign was that of Quemoy and Matsu. In the second of the four debates Senator Kennedy took the position that only the defense of Formosa itself was vital; the vice-president asserted that the two little islands were "in the area of freedom" and insisted that their fall or evacuation would start a chain reaction.[75] Edward Higgins was quick to supply Kennedy's staff with copies of the correspondence between Green and Eisenhower, and early in the next confrontation the Democratic nominee, to his opponent's discomfiture, quoted President Eisenhower's assurance to Green that "neither you nor any other

American need feel that the United States will be involved in military hostilities merely in defense of Quemoy and Matsu." Although the president himself, through his press secretary, insisted that the sentence, if read in context, did not suggest any difference between the position taken by the administration on Quemoy and Matsu and that taken by the Republican candidate, the issue came up again in the final debate. Each candidate held to his original position, but the letters that Higgins had made available had given the Democratic challenger an advantage, as Kennedy acknowledged when he thanked Green's shrewd assistant.[76]

The work load of the Foreign Relations Committee was heavy when Senator Green was its chairman in 1957 and 1958. Although he reached the age of ninety-one near the end of this period, his physical and mental powers appear to have been adequate to the task. During these two years he presided over all but about a dozen of the 184 meetings held by the committee and attended some fifty meetings of subcommittees of which, as chairman of the parent committee, he was an ex-officio member. Although slightly built and apparently frail, he was extraordinarily vigorous. He performed exercises daily, swam, and, whenever it was possible to do so, walked rather than rode. He amazed his colleagues with his endurance on the long trips he made as a Foreign Relations Committee member, in the course of which, besides paying meticulous attention to committee business, he would climb mountains, bathe in cold streams, and attend countless social engagements.[77]

He presided over committee meetings with fairness, dignity, and efficiency. He insisted that briefings of the group by representatives of the executive branch be more frequent and candid, and successfully demanded that his colleagues pay more attention to appointments at the lower level of the foreign service. He and other liberal associates tried, though unsuccessfully, to enforce more committee surveillance over the activities of the Central Intelligence Agency. In 1955 and again in 1958, when he was chairman, he supported broad investigations of CIA operations.[78]

In the late summer of 1958, however, the senator reluctantly began to wear a hearing aid, and his eyesight, impaired by cataracts, also began to fail. In early December—after the midterm elections in which the Democrats retained control of the Senate, thus assuring the Rhode Islander's continuation as Foreign Relations chairman—he told Higgins that he was no longer confident of his ability to discharge his responsibilities and asked Higgins to consult Lyndon Johnson about the procedure for resigning the chairmanship. Green had decided on a step for which there was no recent precedent, and Johnson was able to persuade him only to agree to postpone his resignation until the start of the 1959 session.

Although at one point it seemed as if Johnson's office had leaked the impending resignation—it was stoutly denied by the Texan's staff—the majority leader clearly was reluctant to see Green resign. The next Democrat in line for the chairmanship, Senator Fulbright of Arkansas, was a much stronger critic of American foreign policy than Green and would not be nearly as co-operative as Green had been in carrying out a bipartisan foreign policy. Indeed, Johnson even more than Green believed that foreign affairs policy making was a White House prerogative and that the Senate should accept presidential leadership, and in 1957 he had clashed with Fulbright over the role of the upper chamber, in a dispute occasioned by the Eisenhower administration's Middle East policy. Johnson also needed the vote and support of John McClellan, the other senator from Arkansas, another Democrat, who would be eclipsed by Fulbright's accession to the coveted Foreign Relations Committee chairmanship.[79]

If Green had considered reversing his decision or even postponing his resignation, the issue was settled late in January by a

Providence Journal editorial demanding his resignation.[80] On 29 January, in a letter to Johnson, he formally asked to be relieved of the chairmanship. His decision to resign, he told Johnson, was "based upon serious considerations as to what would be best for my Country, for the United States Senate and for the Senate Committee on Foreign Relations itself . . . the three objects which, as you know, are my chief interests in life."[81]

On the afternoon of 30 January 1959, the Senate Foreign Relations Committee met in a special executive session, at which Lyndon Johnson was present. Copies of Green's letter of resignation had been prepared for distribution to the press at the end of the meeting.[82] The ninety-one-year-old Rhode Islander, acting as chairman for the last time, sat at the head of the table. After the majority leader's speech praising Green had been heard and after a unanimous resolution asking Green to continue as chairman had been firmly declined, the resignation was officially accepted, and the majority leader announced that he would present the name of J. William Fulbright of Arkansas, the next ranking Democrat, to the Senate as the committee's new chairman.

The final two years of Green's senate term passed quietly, as his steps grew a little slower, his hearing a little poorer, and his sight a little dimmer. In January 1960, a year after he had stepped down from the chairmanship, he announced that he had renounced his often-proclaimed goal of reaching the age of 100 while serving as a United States senator, that he would not be a candidate for a fifth term. Claiborne Pell having been elected to succeed him in the Senate, Green's Washington years ended in January 1961 with the inauguration of President Kennedy.

Afterword

THEODORE FRANCIS GREEN saw himself both as custodian of the liberal and humanitarian record of his ancestors and as continuer of their tradition of public service. Aloof Yankee patrician though he was, he was nonetheless profoundly sympathetic to those less privileged than himself, whose lot he believed it the obligation of the individual politician as well as the government to ameliorate. Mixed with his progressivism, his strong attachment to the New Deal, and his sensitivity to the needs of the less fortunate, however, was a strong traditionalist streak. In this he resembled his political mentor, Franklin D. Roosevelt: both came from patrician stock, adopted the role of champion of the underdog, were influenced by the liberalism—and internationalism—of Woodrow Wilson, and had a marked sympathy for people; but both remained aloof in their dealings with individuals, never fully revealing their thoughts. Both were reformers who cherished the heritage of the past and sought to graft necessary changes onto that heritage. Both found it difficult to grasp developments and needs that they could not relate to the heritage they had sprung from.

In his later years, for example, Green was considered a conservative, if not reactionary, influence on his alma mater, Brown University. When the university sought to sever its Baptist connection, he objected vigorously, not because he was intolerant of other denominations and not because he feared that Brown would be dominated by some other creed, but because he was reluctant to break Brown's Baptist tradition, which stemmed from Roger Williams, whom he considered the fountainhead of religious tolerance. When efforts were made to reform the fraternities at Brown, Green also resisted, again from a desire to continue the traditions of the past.

His reformist tendencies were both fostered and inhibited by his sense of tradition. He revered the ideas of Roger Williams, Thomas Wilson Dorr, and those liberal members of his family whose heritage he sought to carry on. He was the fifth member of his family to sit in Congress. "Not me. Write about my family, about what my ancestors did for Rhode Island, the country, and for democracy," he characteristically urged the author.

Green was in many ways the model of a patrician in politics. Political and financial scandal never touched him. A wealthy man who funded his own campaigns rather than be indebted to others for support, he was able to preserve the detached integrity on which statesmanship should rest. Although he sought prestige and savored the recognition that he achieved during his long career, he observed the proper limits of power and never pursued it for its own sake.

It cannot be fairly argued that the people of Rhode Island fared badly because of Green's advanced age. Although he was seventy years old when he first went to Washington, his office was well run, groups and interests from his state were assiduously served, and his voice was respected in the councils of the nation. And through his seniority he achieved a position of considerable influence in Congress, thereby carrying on a tradition that—thanks to the ability as well as to the long tenure of Rhode Island's members of Congress—has enabled the smallest state in the Union to carry weight in Washington disproportionate to its size.

Green's life was purposeful and tranquil, and it is not surprising that Marcus Aurelius's *Meditations* was one of his favorite books. When, after due reflection, Green had decided on a course of action, he set out single-mindedly to achieve his goal. Sometimes his dedication made him abrasive and cantankerous, even to those closest to him. Convinced of the rectitude of his opinions, he was not beset by the doubts that plague so many in politics. Had he not been so deeply schooled in the philosophy of liberalism, in whose humane and tolerant tenets he deeply believed, he might have been doctrinaire and inflexible. But because of those liberal beliefs, he was able to combine an intellectual's logic and moral certainty with a practicing politician's pragmatism and respect for the views of others.

If at the time of his death on 20 May 1966 Theodore Francis Green may have been best known as the oldest man to have served in Congress, his right to a place in history is based on more solid foundations—his consistent liberalism, his intellectual honesty, his internationalism, his insistence that government have compassion for all men, and his long career of faithful public service.

Notes and
Index

Notes

Abbreviations

GP Green Papers, Manuscript Division, Library of Congress, Washington, D.C. An arabic number following indicates the container in which the material is filed.

CW Collected Writings of Theodore Francis Green, John Hay Library, Brown University, Providence, R.I. The folder in which the material appears is indicated by an arabic volume number.

CR U.S., Congress, Senate, *Congressional Record.*

1. President's Man

1. GP 1037.

2. *CR,* app., 22 Feb. 1937, pp. 279–81. One suspects that the White House either instigated this Green effort or was at least enthusiastically acquiescent. Four days later the president wrote that the speech was "grand" and told the senator how much he appreciated his eloquent support (Franklin D. Roosevelt to Green, 25 Feb. 1937 [GP 1037]).

3. Mrs. Brown to Green, 11 Feb. and 6 Mar. 1937; Green to Mrs. Brown, 13 Feb. and 10 Mar. 1937 (GP 35).

4. J. E. Bacon to Green, 1 Mar. 1937; Green to Bacon, 3 Mar. 1937 (GP 35).

5. *CR,* 12 Mar. 1937, pp. 2136–37.

6. Speech before National Lawyers Guild, New York, 30 Apr. 1937 (GP 1037).

7. Chafee to Green, 15 June 1937 (GP 35).

8. Roosevelt to Green, 23 July 1937 (GP 1037).

9. See Erwin L. Levine, *Theodore Francis Green: The Rhode Island Years, 1906–1936* (Providence, 1963), pp. 145–95.

10. Johnson to Green, 24 June 1937 (GP 35).

11. J. T. Witherow to Green, 13 Sept. 1937 (GP 35).

12. Richard Polenburg, *Reorganizing Roosevelt's Government: The Controversy over Executive Reorganization, 1936–1939* (Cambridge, Mass., 1966), p. 28.

13. U.S., Congress, Senate, Special Committee to Investigate Lobbying Activities, *Hearings,* 75th Cong., 3d sess., pt. 7, 18 Mar. 1938, pp. 2113–21, and 23 Mar. 1937, pp. 2161–69.

14. J. L. Jenks to Green, 24 Mar. 1938; Green to Jenks, 25 Mar. 1938; Green to R. Adams, 25 Mar. 1938; Charles W. Lippitt to Green, 28 Mar. 1938; Green to Lippitt, 28 Mar. 1938; Chafee to Green, 26 Mar. 1938; Green to Chafee, 31 Mar. 1938 (GP 37).

15. Green to G. S. Burgess, 30 Mar. 1938 (GP 36).

16. Radio address, 27 Aug. 1937 (CW 3).

17. "Round Table Discussion with the Hon. Theodore Francis Green," CBS, 23 Dec. 1937 (*CR,* app., 21 Jan. 1938, pp. 270–71).

18. GP 1039.

19. *CR,* app., 23 May 1938, pp. 2097–98.

20. Chafee to Green, 20 Jan. 1943 (GP 263).

21. Green to Chafee, 25 Jan. 1943 (GP 263).

22. Green to Mrs. Henry Brandyce, 1 Feb. 1943 (GP 263).

23. Green to Mrs. Harry E. Yarnell, 1 Feb. 1943 (GP 263).

2. New Dealer

1. See *CR,* 28 Aug. 1941, p. 7238, and 11 Feb. 1942, p. 1189.

2. *CR,* 11 Jan. 1943, p. 72.

3. *CR,* app., 21 Jan. 1943, pp. A236–38.

4. In concluding a radio talk in support of social security reform, Green said: "When peace comes at last, we will have discovered that a wealth of material things, such as America has boasted of in the past, is not enough. We must consider the needs of all classes and kinds of people and we must serve them. There will not be enough wealth in the world to save us if it is indiscriminately packed as so much cargo on one side of the ship, unbalanced. We shall pitch over, and the gorged and the hungry will go down together. But balanced and rationally distributed for the rightful sharing of all, our cargo

will keep and nourish and prosper all of us, the lesser as well as the greater, the last as well as the first. This means social security" (*CR*, app., 21 Jan. 1943, p. A238). From this it would seem that Green not only had a surprisingly advanced concept of social security legislation for the United States but that he was also ahead of his time in his awareness of the dangers of economic imbalance between developed and developing nations.

5. *CR*, 25 June 1945, p. 6635.

6. *CR*, 7 May 1947, pp. 4652, 4651.

7. Ibid., p. 4654.

8. Rhode Island State Industrial Council study, 6–7 Dec. 1947, p. 12 (GP 1046).

9. Statement by Franklin D. Roosevelt, 31 Aug. 1935 (*Documents, Peace and War, United States Foreign Policy, 1931–1941* [Washington, 1943], p. 272).

10. Green to A. W. Hunt, 16 May 1938 (GP 39).

11. Green's office compiled a list of pro-Loyalist individuals and groups (GP 39). Some Loyalist supporters wrote to Green to point out that they were not automatically to be branded as Communists or radicals (R. L. Paddock, American Friends of Spanish Democracy, to Green, 3 May 1938 [GP 39]). For pro-Catholic sentiment, see GP 81–85 and 89–95.

12. Green to Harry Sherman, 12 Jan. 1939 (GP 89).

13. Green to D. B. Kiely, 6 Feb. 1939 (GP 80).

14. U.S., Congress, Senate Foreign Relations Committee, *Hearings on Neutrality, Peace Legislation, and Our Foreign Policy,* 76th Cong., 1st sess., 1 May 1939, p. 390; office memorandum, 5 July 1939 (GP 90).

15. Speech at Crescent Park, R.I., 10 Sept. 1939 (GP 1039).

16. See *CR*, app., 27 Oct. 1939, pp. 563–64.

17. Press release, 23 Aug. 1940 (GP 130).

18. *CR*, app., 23 Feb. 1941, pp. A797–98.

19. Cordell Hull, *The Memoirs of Cordell Hull* (New York, 1948), p. 1047; U.S., Congress, Senate Foreign Relations Committee, *Hearings on Modification of Neutrality Act of 1939*, 77th Cong., 1st sess., 21–24 Oct. 1941, pp. 13, 48–62, 223–27.

20. Franklin D. Roosevelt, *Nothing to Fear: The Selected Addresses of Franklin D. Roosevelt, 1932–1945,* ed. B. D. Zevin (Boston, 1946), p. 299.

21. *CR*, 1 Nov. 1941, pp. 8402–4.

22. U.S., Congress, Senate Appropriations Committee, Subcommittee on Manpower Investigation, *Hearings*, 78th Cong., 1st sess., pts. 1 and 2, 28 Jan. to 22 Feb. 1943 and 26 Feb. to 2 Mar. 1943.

23. "The Size of Our Army," *CR*, app., 1 Mar. 1943, A855–56. See also *CR*, app., 4 Mar. 1943, pp. A1012–18.

24. GP 1043.

25. Marshall to Green, 11 Apr. 1943 (GP 269).

26. *CR*, 1 Feb. 1951, pp. 860–61.

27. *CR*, 12 June 1952, pp. 7119–28; *CR*, 13 June 1952, p. 7175; *CR*, 16 June 1952, pp. 7238–71; *CR*, 18 June 1952, pp. 7463–66.

28. S. 2298, *CR*, 2 May 1939, p. 4995. U.S., Congress, Senate Committee on Banking and Currency, *Hearings on S. 2298*, 76th Cong., 1st sess., 7 June 1939.

29. U.S., Congress, Senate Committee on Banking and Currency, *Hearings on S. 2298*, 76th Cong., 1st sess., 7 June 1939.

30. *Providence Journal*, 8 June 1939, p. 10.

31. Green to Vanderbilt, 3 Nov. 1939 (GP 127).

32. GP 81.

33. Vernon Norton to Green, 6 Nov. 1939 (GP 81).

34. Published as *New England's Textile Future* (Providence, 1948).

35. GP 558.

36. Green to Truman, 3 Aug. 1949 (GP 1124).

37. Memorandum, 6 Oct. 1949; Green to Truman, 11 Oct. 1949; Hoffman to Green, 11 and 21 Oct. 1949; John McCormack to Higgins, 20 Oct. 1949; Higgins to Truman, 2 Nov. 1949 (GP 591).

38. Wriston to Green, 12 Dec. 1957 (GP 896).

39. Green to Charles C. Fichtner, 16 Jan. 1958 (GP 911).

3. Representative

1. See Sylvia Porter, "Twelve Men against the Nation: No Silver Bullets for Our Guns," *Barron's National Business and Financial Weekly*, 5 Oct. 1942, p. 3; Herbert M. Bratton, "Contention of Silver Advocates Prior to Passage of the Silver Purchase Act of 1934," reprinted in *CR*, 2 May 1940, pp. 5387–93; *CR*, 1 May 1940, p. 5305; *CR*, app., 26 Feb. 1940, pp. 986–88.

2. *CR,* 17 Jan. 1939, p. 407; *CR,* 30 Apr. 1940, pp. 5248–49; *CR,* 1 May 1940, pp. 5300–18; *CR,* 2 May 1940, pp. 5383–5401; *CR,* 9 May 1940, p. 5826.

3. Memoranda and notes relevant to the silver issue and its effect on Rhode Island can be found in GP 1118–22.

4. *Providence Journal,* 31 July 1942, p. 11.

5. Ibid., p. 1.

6. Edward O. Otis, Jr., executive secretary of the New England Manufacturing Jewelers' and Silversmiths' Association, to Green, 19 July 1942; Otis to James E. Murray, 13 July 1942 (GP 1120).

7. *Providence Journal,* 31 July 1942, p. 10. See also ibid., 31 Mar. 1942, pp. 1, 7; 1 Apr. 1942, pp. 1, 3; and 2 Apr. 1942, pp. 1, 3; 30 July 1942, pp. 1, 4.

8. W. G. Meader to Christopher Del Sesto, state director of the Office of Price Administration, Rhode Island, 12 Aug. 1942 (GP 1120); *Providence Journal,* 17 Aug. 1942, pp. 1, 2.

9. W. S. Murphy to Green, 5 Aug. 1942 (GP 1120).

10. *CR,* 14 Sept. 1942, p. 7117. Green's bill was known as S. 2768. See U.S., Congress, Subcommittee of the Senate Banking and Currency Committee, *Hearings on S. 2768,* 77th Cong., 2d sess., 14 Oct. 1942, pp. 9–15.

11. *CR,* 17 Sept. 1942, p. 7182.

12. Frederick A. Ballou, Jr., to Green, 29 Sept. 1942; Thurber to Green, 24 Sept. 1942; Frank Lilly to Green, 21 and 29 Sept. 1942 (GP 1120). *New York Times,* 20 Sept. 1942, p. 16.

13. Spahr to Green, 19 Sept. 1942; Green to Charles J. Michaels, 10 Oct. 1942 (GP 1120).

14. Nelson to Robert F. Wagner, 10 Oct. 1942; Green to Francis Maloney, 14 Oct. 1942 (GP 1120).

15. U.S., Congress, Subcommittee of the Senate Banking and Currency Committee, *Hearings on S. 2768,* 77th Cong., 2d sess., 14 Oct. 1942, pp. 9–15.

16. S. Rept. 1770, 77th Cong., 2d sess., 3 Dec. 1942.

17. *CR,* 7 Dec. 1942, p. 9355.

18. "Drafting Silver for the War," panel discussion on "American Forum of the Air," Mutual Broadcasting System, 3 Jan. 1943 (CW 3).

19. *CR,* 7 Jan. 1943, p. 34 (Green's S. 35); *CR,* 7 Jan. 1943, p. 36 (Murdock's S. 192); *CR,* 26 Apr. 1943, p. 3737 (McCarran's S. 1036).

20. U.S., Congress, Senate Subcommittee on Coinage and Related

Matters, *Hearings on S. 35, S. 192, and S. 1036,* 78th Cong., 1st sess., 28 and 29 Apr. 1943; S. Rept. 223, *CR,* 12 May 1943, p. 4247; *New York Times,* 12 May 1943, p. 27. For content of bill as recommended by the subcommittee, see *CR,* 18 June 1943, p. 6057.

21. *CR,* 17 May 1943, p. 4503; *CR,* 20 May 1943, p. 4660; *CR,* 18 June 1943, p. 6058.

22. *CR,* 5 July 1943, pp. 7213–17.

23. *Providence Journal,* 13 July 1943, p. 14.

24. Donald Nelson to Green, 15 Nov. 1943; Green to Walter E. Spahr, 19 Nov. 1943 (GP 1119). *New York Times,* 18 Nov. 1943, p. 34. *Providence Journal,* 8 Dec. 1943, p. 14.

25. *CR,* 9 Feb. 1944, pp. 1499, 1488.

26. *CR,* 29 May 1944, p. 5074; *CR,* 29 Nov. 1944, pp. 8559–60; *CR,* app., 1 Apr. 1944, pp. A1716–17. See also S. Rept. 1230, 78th Cong., 2d sess., 28 Nov. 1944.

27. *CR,* 20 June 1945, p. 6322.

28. S. 1508, *CR,* 24 Oct. 1945, p. 9938.

29. *Evening Bulletin* (Providence), 14 Dec. 1945, p. 14. Bowles to Robert F. Wagner, 13 Dec. 1945; Small to Wagner, 17 Dec. 1945; Fred Vinson to Wagner, 27 Nov. 1945 (GP 1121).

30. H.R. 4590, *CR,* 5 Nov. 1945, p. 10403; *CR,* 19 Dec. 1945, p. 12368; H. Rept. 1554, 79th Cong., 2d sess., 12 Feb. 1946, p. 9.

31. U.S., Congress, Senate Subcommittee of the Appropriations Committee, *Hearings on H.R. 5452,* 79th Cong., 2d sess., 1947, p. 252.

32. U.S., Congress, Senate Subcommittee on Treasury and Post Office Departments Appropriation Bill, *Hearings on H.R. 5452,* 79th Cong., 2d sess., 1946, p. 329.

33. Memoranda (GP 1122). See also *CR,* 21 June 1946, p. 7289.

34. *CR,* 9 July 1946, p. 8495.

35. *Providence Journal,* 11 July 1946, p. 1.

36. *CR,* 12 July 1946, p. 8751.

37. *CR,* 15 July 1946, p. 8982; *CR,* 19 July 1946, pp. 9420, 9477; *CR,* 23 July 1946, p. 9800; *CR,* 31 July 1946, p. 10636.

38. McChesney to Green, 25 July 1946 (GP 1122). See also *Executive Jeweler* 1 (June 1946): 39; Edward O. Otis, Jr., to Green, 6 June 1946; and Frederick A. Ballou to Green, 2 Aug. 1946 (GP 1122).

39. *CR,* 6 Jan. 1947, p. 125; *CR,* 27 Jan. 1947, pp. 599–600; *CR,* 31 Jan. 1947, p. 719; *CR,* 3 Feb. 1947, p. 737; *CR,* 7 Apr. 1947, p. 3143. See also Oscar Chapman to Green, 14 Feb. 1947 (GP 1115).

40. Higgins to McChesney, 17 Jan. 1947; McChesney to Higgins, 27 Jan. 1947; Green to McChesney, 3 Feb. 1947; McChesney to Green, 20 Feb. 1947; Green to W. L. Clayton, 24 Jan. 1947; Clayton to Green, 6 Feb. 1947 (GP 1115).

41. McChesney to Higgins, 29 Oct. 1947; McChesney to Green, 11 Feb. 1948 (GP 1116).

42. McChesney to Green, 4 Dec. 1947; John Snyder to Green, 26 Nov. 1947 (GP 1115).

43. "The Silver Scandal," radio address, WJAR, Providence, R.I., 14 Oct. 1948 (CW 4).

44. Office memorandum, 19 Dec. 1949 (GP 1116).

45. S. 2829, *CR*, 11 Jan. 1950, p. 290.

46. Higgins to Green, 3 Jan. 1950; memorandum, 11 Jan. 1950 (GP 1116). See also U.S., Congress, Joint Committee on the Economic Report, *Report of the Senate Subcommittee on Monetary, Credit, and Fiscal Policies,* 81st Cong., 2d sess., pp. 40–41, and press release of Economists' National Committee on Monetary Policy, 6 Mar. 1950. Forand's bill was H.R. 6724, *CR*, 12 Jan. 1950, p. 366.

47. *New York Times,* 13 Feb. 1950, p. 10.

48. Ibid., 8 Jan. 1955, p. 15.

49. *CR,* 14 Mar. 1955, p. 2777. See also *New York Times,* 16 July 1955, p. 19.

50. U.S., Congress, Senate Subcommittee of the Committee on Banking and Currency, *Hearings on S. 1427,* 84th Cong., 1st sess., 1955, pt. 1, p. 104.

51. Ibid., pp. 55–71, 78–87, 103–11, 292–99.

52. *Providence Journal,* 7 June 1956, pp. 1, 16.

4. Legislator

1. *CR,* 20 July 1942, p. 6423; *CR,* 22 July 1942, p. 6480; *CR,* 17 Aug. 1942, p. 6858; *CR,* 20 Aug. 1942, p. 6891.

2. *CR,* 23 July 1942, pp. 6541–69.

3. *CR,* 17 Aug. 1942, pp. 6858–65; *CR,* 20 Aug. 1942, p. 6882; *CR,* 24 Aug. 1942, pp. 6923–38.

4. *CR,* 25 Aug. 1942, pp. 6962–72.

5. *CR,* 22 Nov. 1943, p. 9792.

6. For a brief review of the chaotic situation in the states regarding the diverse laws on absentee voting, see Robert Cutler, *No Time for Rest* (Boston, 1966), pp. 168–69. See also a speech on the subject by Representative Eugene Worley (*CR,* 18 Dec. 1943, pp. 10908–9).

7. *CR,* 29 June 1943, p. 6690; *CR,* 30 June 1943, p. 6894.

8. *CR,* 12 Oct. 1943, p. 8228.

9. See radio address, "The Soldiers' Vote Bill," WHN, New York, 15 Nov. 1943 (CW 3).

10. *New York Times,* 10 Nov. 1943, p. 16.

11. *CR,* 22 Nov. 1943, pp. 9791, 9812–18.

12. *CR,* 29 Nov. 1943, p. 10080.

13. *CR,* 30 Nov. 1943, p. 10133.

14. *CR,* 1 Dec. 1943, p. 10178.

15. *CR,* 22 Nov. 1943, p. 9818; *CR,* 2 Dec. 1943, p. 10218.

16. *CR,* 29 Nov. 1943, p. 10064.

17. *CR,* 1 Dec. 1943, p. 10172.

18. See Higgins to Francis Kiernan, 4 Dec. 1943 (GP 348) and Allen Drury, *A Senate Journal, 1943–1945* (New York, 1963), p. 12.

19. *New York Times,* 5 Dec. 1943, p. L–48; 12 Dec. 1943, pp. L–9, E–3. See also Drury, p. 21.

20. *New York Times,* 10 Dec. 1943, p. 18.

21. Ibid., 12 Dec. 1943, p. L–9.

22. Ibid., 19 Dec. 1943, p. 4.

23. Ibid., 15 Jan. 1944, pp. 1, 26.

24. Ibid., 18 Jan. 1944, p. 40.

25. Ibid., 6 Jan. 1944, pp. 1, 13; 7 Jan. 1955, p. 18; 13 Jan. 1944, pp. 1, 11; 15 Jan. 1944, p. 26.

26. *CR,* 11 Jan. 1944, p. 28; *CR,* 24 Jan. 1944, pp. 604–6.

27. George Sokolsky, in the *Baltimore Sun,* 24 Jan. 1944 (GP 347).

28. *CR,* 24 Jan. 1944, p. 612.

29. Ibid., pp. 606–24.

30. *CR,* 26 Jan. 1944, pp. 706–8.

31. Ibid., p. 713.

32. *CR,* 27 Jan. 1944, pp. 812–14.

33. *CR,* 28 Jan. 1944, p. 895; *CR,* 3 Feb. 1944, p. 1229. See also *New York Times,* 2 Feb. 1944, pp. 1, 12.

34. *CR,* 1 Feb. 1944, p. 1044; *CR,* 2 Feb. 1944, p. 1069.

35. Roy Wilkins to Green, 2 Feb. 1944 (GP 349).

36. *CR,* 4 Feb. 1944, p. 1252.

37. Ibid., p. 1266.

38. *CR,* 7 Feb. 1944, pp. 1291–92; *CR,* 8 Feb. 1944, pp. 1387–1406.

39. *New York Times,* 10 Feb. 1944, pp. 1, 34; 11 Feb. 1944, pp. 1, 34.

40. Ibid., 1 Mar. 1944, pp. 1, 34. Green to Anne Marsoli, 8 Mar. 1944; Green to Leo Zwell, 15 Mar. 1944 (GP 349).

41. *CR,* 13 Mar. 1944, p. 2499.

42. *CR,* 14 Mar. 1944, p. 2573; *CR,* 15 Mar. 1944, p. 2639.

43. *New York Times,* 16 Mar. 1944, pp. 1, 36; *CR,* 31 Mar. 1944, pp. 3356–57.

44. S. 1828, *CR,* 1 Apr. 1944, p. 3380.

45. *CR,* 13 Apr. 1944, p. 3432.

46. See *New York Times,* 2 Aug. 1944, p. 1, and 10 Aug. 1944, pp. 1, 15; *Saturday Review of Literature,* 29 July 1944, p. 12.

47. S. 2050, *CR,* 1 Aug. 1944, p. 6704; *CR,* 15 Aug. 1944, p. 6939; *CR,* 22 Aug. 1944, p. 7167.

48. U.S., Congress, S. Rept. 1065, 79th Cong., 2d sess., 15 Mar. 1946, p. 2.

49. *Voting in the Armed Services,* H. Doc. 407, 82d Cong., 2d sess., 28 Mar. 1952, pp. 1, 25–27.

5. Politician

1. Interview with Senator John Sparkman of Alabama, 10 May 1966.

2. Interview with Pastore, 3 Feb. 1966.

3. Higgins to William Maguire, Rhode Island director of Federal Emergency Public Works Administration, 8 July 1937 (GP 10).

4. McKellar to Green, 11 Jan. 1937; Green to McKellar, 15 Jan. 1937 (GP 9).

5. Interview with Higgins.

6. Memorandum of conference with Franklin D. Roosevelt, 6 June 1937 (GP 10). Interview with Higgins. A young man from North Kingstown, Rhode Island, Rowland Hazard, who was placed through Green as a mail carrier, began a long government career that eventu-

ally brought him to the Canal Zone as United States Attorney; Green and Higgins carefully paved the way for each step of his advancement (Green to Hayden, 6 July 1937 [GP 10]).

7. Office memoranda, 26 Sept. 1946 (GP 1124). Interview with Higgins.

8. Green to Frank Murphy, 29 Apr. 1939; memorandum of a conference with Murphy, 11 Oct. 1939; Vernon Norton to Thomas G. Corcoran, 17 Nov. 1939; Green to Roosevelt, 2 Oct. 1939; Green to Ashurst, 1 Nov. 1939; Matthew Maguire to Green, 11 Dec. 1939; Higgins to Green, 1 Dec. 1939; William H. Vanderbilt to Hartigan, 11 Jan. 1940 (GP 134). *Providence Journal*, 25 Feb. 1940, p. 2. *Evening Bulletin* (Providence), 24 Feb. 1940, pp. 1, 6.

9. Erwin L. Levine, *Theodore Francis Green: The Rhode Island Years, 1906–1936* (Providence, 1963), pp. 156–58, 165–67. Green to Roosevelt, Green to Cummings, and Green to Farley, 31 Dec. 1937; T. Luongo to Green, 15 July 1937; James J. McCabe to Green, 31 July 1937; T. D. Quinn to Green, 3 Nov. 1937; Higgins to Green, 15 Nov. 1937; Luigi de Pasquale to Green, 12 Feb. 1938; Higgins to Green, 3 Jan. 1938 (GP 80).

10. The Democratic candidate for governor, J. Howard McGrath, needed an Italian-American on the ticket, and Dennis Roberts, then the mayor of Providence, championed Pastore rather than Christopher Del Sesto. The latter, a capable young Democrat for whom Green and Higgins had procured patronage, had at one time been grateful for Green's assistance (Del Sesto to Green, 6 Mar. 1941 [GP 173]); after the senator backed Pastore, however, Del Sesto angrily left the Democratic party. Pastore, who became the first Italian-American governor in the nation when McGrath resigned the governorship to join the Department of Justice, thus began his journey to the United States Senate. Del Sesto, running as a Republican in 1958, finally became governor by defeating the incumbent, Roberts.

11. Higgins to Green, 27 Aug. 1937; E. K. Burlew to Green, 8 Sept. 1937; Green to Roosevelt, 18 Sept. 1937; Marvin McIntyre to Green, 28 Sept. 1937; Green to James Dunne, 9 Oct. 1937 (GP 9).

12. James H. Kiernan to Green, 25 June 1937; Green to E. K. Burlew, 28 June 1937; Green to Albertus Hazard, 23 Aug. 1937; memorandum of meeting of Green with Farrell Coyle, WPA administrator for Rhode Island, and R. A. Huppach, National Park Service, 13 Dec. 1937; Green to H. C. Hoxci, 13 Dec. 1937 (GP 1). Burlew to

Higgins, 23 Aug. and 17 Sept. 1938; H. A. Gray to Green, 9, 10, and 15 Sept. 1938 and 6, 7, 8, 17, and 29 Oct. 1938; Higgins to Marie Flanagan, 8 Mar. 1938 (GP 52).

13. Peter McManus to Higgins, 12 Feb. 1937; McManus to Green, 16 Mar. 1937; Robert Fechner to Aime Forand, 16 Mar. 1937; General W. H. Wilson to Green, 18 Mar. 1937; McManus to Green, 19 Mar. 1937; McManus to Higgins, 7 Sept. 1937; John E. Fogarty to Green, 6 Dec. 1937 (GP 1). McManus to Higgins, 10 Feb. 1938; Higgins to McManus, 31 Mar. 1938; Higgins to J. Rossi, 17 Oct. 1938 (GP 52).

14. J. P. Adams to Green, 23 Jan. 1939; memorandum from Gordon Harrison to Green, 16 Sept. 1939; Wriston to Green, 16 Oct. 1939; Wriston to Bureau of Navigation, 6 Nov. 1939; Green to Franklin D. Roosevelt, 10 Sept. 1940; James Forrestal to Green, 11 Sept. 1940 (GP 216). Interview with Higgins.

15. Interview with Higgins.

16. Secretary of the Navy Claude A. Swanson to William G. Bankhead, Speaker of the House, 27 Dec. 1938, in H. Doc. 65, 76th Cong., 1st sess., p. 11. Interview with Higgins.

17. The *Providence Journal* not only featured Sandager's attack but also expressed doubts about the necessity for establishing a base in Rhode Island.

18. Franklin D. Roosevelt to Green, 12 Jan. 1939; Green to William H. Vanderbilt, 16 Jan. 1939; Edison to Green, 4 Mar. 1939; Vanderbilt to Green, 11 and 17 Jan. 1939 (GP 74). *Providence Sunday Journal,* 29 Jan. 1939, sec. 2, p. 2. See also GP 73.

19. *CR,* 25 Jan. 1939, p. 742; *CR,* 18 May 1939, p. 5702. Green to James Carr, 10 Apr. 1939; Green to Brigadier General H. R. Deane, adjutant of Rhode Island, 10 Apr. 1939; radio address, WEAN, Providence, R.I., 21 Apr. 1939 (GP 74).

20. S. 2975, *CR,* 2 Oct. 1939, p. 47. Office memoranda, 1, 7, and 8 Nov. 1939; Green to Admiral Ben Moreell, 6 Dec. 1939; Higgins to Charles Maguire, 13 Dec. 1939; Charles Edison to Green, 9 Dec. 1939; Green to David I. Walsh, 17 May 1940; Green to James F. Byrnes, 21 May 1940; Green to Carl Vinson, 17 May 1940; Walsh to Green, 21 May 1940; Vinson to Green, 18 May 1940 (GP 127). H.R. 8533, *CR,* 19 Feb. 1940, p. 1673. Roosevelt to Moreell, 18 June 1940; Harry A. Smith to Higgins, 8 Aug. 1940 (GP 127). See also Higgins to Edward J. Flynn, 17 Sept. 1940; Marie Flanagan to Green, 3 Aug. 1940; Fran-

ces Cohen to Higgins, 18 July 1940; Green to Crandall, 31 July 1940; Higgins to Green, 1 Aug. 1940; Green to Crandall, 1 Aug. 1940 (GP 127).

21. *CR,* 27 Mar. 1941, pp. 2610–11.

22. A. L. Richard to Green, 20 Apr. 1937; Green to Edison, 26 Apr. 1937; Edison to Green, 29 Apr. 1937; Kingsley to Green, 4 June and 15 Nov. 1937 (GP 7).

23. Memorandum, Cornelius C. Moore to Green, 13 Nov. 1937; Thomas McCoy to Green, 21 May 1938; Green to Roosevelt, 21 Nov. 1938; Roosevelt to Green, 3 Dec. 1938 (GP 8).

24. Interview with Higgins.

25. Memoranda, 29 Nov. and 16 Dec. 1937; Green to Charles Benheimer, secretary, Jamestown (R.I.) Board of Trade, 17 Dec. 1937 (GP 7). Roosevelt to Green, 8 Mar. 1938 (GP 64).

26. Green to C. A. Curley, secretary, Newport Metal Trades Council, 8 Mar. 1938; Claude A. Swanson to Green, 21 Apr. 1938 (GP 64).

27. Memorandum, Green to Higgins, 18 May 1945 (GP 365).

28. See U.S., Congress, Senate Committee on Naval Affairs, *Hearings on Proposed Transfer of Certain Manufacturing Activities from the Newport Naval Training Station to Forest Park, Illinois,* 79th Cong., 1st sess., 11 Dec. 1945. James Forrestal to Green, 26 Dec. 1945; Green, Peter G. Gerry, Aime Forand, and John E. Fogarty to Harry S. Truman, 4 Feb. 1946; Matthew Connolly to Forand, 15 Feb. 1946; Cornelius C. Moore to Green, 13 Dec. 1945 (GP 394). *CR,* 18 Jan. 1959, p. 11257. Interview with Higgins.

29. U.S., Congress, Subcommittee of Senate Appropriations Committee, *Hearings,* 79th Cong., 2d sess., 4 June 1946, pp. 169–284. *CR,* 21 June 1946, pp. 7396–7407.

30. U.S., Congress, House Civil Service Committee, *Hearings on H.R. 4718: Retirement after Twenty-five Years of Service,* 79th Cong., 2d sess., 11 June 1946, p. 79. S. 1422, *CR,* 24 Sept. 1945, p. 8882. Green to Chester Spaats, president, Federal Employees' Retirement Association, Narragansett Bay Area, 22 July 1946; Spaats to Green, 16 July 1946; S. C. Malphus to Green, 30 July 1946 (GP 400).

31. S. 2366, S. Rept. 1678, 79th Cong., 2d sess., 10 July 1946. W. John Kenney, assistant secretary of the navy, to Green, 17 Jan. 1947; Higgins to James Maher, 10 Aug. 1949 (GP 400).

32. Hines to Green, 28 July 1938; Hines to Green, 31 July 1940; Higgins to J. Howard McGrath, 31 July 1940; Hines to Green, 24 Mar. 1941; Hines to Green, 23 Feb. 1943 (GP 1130).

33. Memoranda, 9 Feb. 1944; Roosevelt to Green, 13 Mar. 1944; Hines to Green, 19 Aug. 1944. Green to Bradley, 5 Nov. 1945; Bradley to Green, 7 Nov. 1945; Marie Flanagan to Higgins, 19 Apr. 1945 (GP 1130). For memoranda between Higgins and Sullivan, see GP 559.

34. *CR,* 14 Mar. 1940, p. 2842.

35. Office memoranda, 7, 13, 20 July 1940 (GP 143).

36. *New York American,* 7, 23 Aug. 1940 (GP 130).

37. Address at Bridgeport, Conn., 17 Oct. 1940 (GP 1040).

38. *Providence Journal,* 22 Oct. 1940, pp. 1, 5.

39. U.S., Congress, Subcommittee of the Senate Committee on Interstate Commerce, *Hearings on Investigation of Alleged Wiretapping,* 76th Cong., 3d sess., pts. 1, 2, and 3. See also private memoranda in the personal files of Edward J. Higgins, Warren, R.I.

40. *Providence Sunday Journal,* 11 Jan. 1942, sec. 2, p. 1, and *Providence Journal,* 14 Jan. 1942, p. 13.

41. Ibid., 29 Sept. 1942, p. 9.

42. Ibid., 21 Oct. 1942, p. 3.

43. Campaign address, 25 Oct. 1942 (CW 3).

44. *1943 Journal-Bulletin Almanac* (Providence, 1943), p. 232.

45. GP 1044.

46. McGrath's new position enabled Higgins to procure much extra publicity for Green in the 1948 campaign.

47. *Providence Journal,* 13 May 1947, pp. 1, 2.

48. *CR,* app., 21 May 1947, pp. A2384–85.

49. *CR,* 19 Jan. 1948. Campaign speech, WPRO, Providence, R.I., 3 Nov. 1948; *Railroad Trainman,* 8 Feb. 1948, pp. 50–54; Anthony Valenta, international president, United Textile Workers of America, AFL, to Green, 16 Aug. 1948 (GP 1046).

50. Address at annual convention of Franco-American War Veterans, 9 Oct. 1948, Providence, R.I. (CW 4).

51. Interview with Higgins.

52. *Providence Journal,* 1 June 1954, p. 2; *Providence Sunday Journal,* 18 July 1954, sec. 1, p. 7; interview with Higgins.

53. Green to Sinclair Weeks, 17 Sept. and 4 Oct. 1954; F. W. Reichelderter, chief of U.S. Weather Bureau, to Green, 8 Sept. 1954; Green to D. M. Little, acting chief of U.S. Weather Bureau, 10 Sept. 1954; Green to Spessard L. Holland, 1 and 7 June, 1955 (GP 743). *CR,* 14 June 1955, p. 8097; *CR,* 16 June 1955, pp. 8449–50.

54. *1955 Journal-Bulletin Almanac* (Providence, 1955), p. 245.

55. *Machinists' Monthly Journal,* Sept. 1954, p. 275.
56. Interview with Higgins.

6. Senate Leader

1. Or at least there was in Green's time; some authorities believe that it is now dying.
2. Interview with Higgins.
3. Ibid.
4. Ibid.
5. Ibid.
6. Johnson to Green, 27 Aug. and 19 Nov. 1954 (GP 788).
7. Walter White to Green, 4 Jan. 1938; Tom Terral to Green, 19 Feb. 1938 (GP 36). *CR,* 16 Feb. 1938, p. 2007.
8. Radio interview, Green and Richard Eaton, 15 June 1943 (GP 1042).
9. *CR,* 15 May 1944, p. 4470. See also U.S., Congress, Senate Committee on Rules and Administration, *Hearings on Rule 22,* 85th Cong., 1st sess., 1957, p. 45.
10. *CR,* 22 Mar. 1951, p. 2843. See U.S., Congress, Senate Rules and Administration Committee, *Hearings on Limitation on Debate in the Senate,* 82d Cong., 1st sess., 1951, and S. Rept. 1256, 82d Cong., 2d sess., 12 Mar. 1952.
11. U.S., Congress, Senate Committee on Rules and Administration, *Hearings on Limitation on Debate in the Senate,* 81st Cong., 1st sess., 1949; S. Rept. 268, 83d Cong., 1st sess., 12 Mar. 1953, p. 12.
12. *CR,* 4 Jan. 1957, p. 215.
13. Memorandum, 5 Jan. 1957, p. 215.
14. S. Rept. 1509, 85th Cong., 2d sess., 30 Apr. 1958.
15. *CR,* 12 Jan. 1959, pp. 439–94.
16. G. Mennen Williams to Green, 3 July 1957; James Carey to Green, 8 July 1937 (GP 890).
17. Rowland Evans and Robert Novak, *Lyndon B. Johnson: The Exercise of Power* (New York, 1966), pp. 134–40.
18. Ibid. A. C. Masterson to Higgins, 26 July 1957; Green to Ruth Switzer, 1 Aug. 1957; Green to William D. Wiley, 2 Aug. 1957; Johnson to Green, 9 Sept. 1957; Green to Johnson, 12 Sept. 1957 (GP 890).

19. Green to T. H. Hare Powel, 12 Jan. 1948 and 11 June 1948 (GP 518).

20. *CR,* 27 June 1952, p. 8267.

21. Press release, 1 Oct. 1950 (GP 603). See also Cabell Phillips, *The Truman Presidency* (New York, 1966), pp. 372–77. Ernest Angell, Patrick Malin, and Arthur Garfield Hayes to Green, 14 Sept. 1950; Lee A. Lemos to Green, 21 Sept. 1950; Green to Lemos, 22 Sept. 1950; Green to Henry D. Lloyd, Jr., 3 Oct. 1950 (GP 603).

22. Copy of a letter from William E. Rine, station manager, to William O. Player, Jr., Department of State, 27 Mar. 1960 (GP 1106). A copy of the text supplied to Green by the radio station that broadcast the speech supports 205.

23. See Earl Latham, *The Communist Conspiracy in Washington: From the New Deal to McCarthy* (Cambridge, Mass, 1966), pp. 269–316.

24. U.S., Congress, Special Subcommittee of the Senate Foreign Relations Committee, *Hearings on S. Res. 231,* 22 Feb. 1950, 81st Cong., 2d sess., pp. 19–23.

25. Ibid., p. 550.

26. Ibid., pp. 1167–82; *New York Daily Mirror,* 22 Apr. 1950 (GP 1111C).

27. See committee print, Senate Foreign Relations Committee, 81st Cong., 2d sess., 15 June 1950. See also *CR,* 15 Aug. 1951, p. 10009. The department promptly complied with the committee's minor suggestions.

28. See *Washington Star,* 18 July 1950 (GP 1108).

29. *CR,* 1 Dec. 1954, pp. 16269–77, 16279–341, 16344–46. See GP 1108 for letters opposing censure.

30. *CR,* app., 5 June 1944, pp. A2795–97.

31. Radio speech, WMAL, Washington, D.C., 12 July 1945 (GP 1045).

32. Herbert W. Briggs, "The UNRRA Agreement and Congress," *American Journal of International Law,* 38 (Oct. 1944): 650–58.

33. Press release, Sayre and Green, 24 Aug. 1943 (GP 1045).

34. Green to Kenneth Colgrove, 31 Aug. 1943 (GP 1126). See also *CR,* 8 July 1943, p. 7436.

35. *Providence Journal,* 19 Aug. 1943, p. 15.

36. The same attitude is evident in Green's opposition to the requirement of a two-thirds vote to impose cloture, discussed earlier in this chapter.

37. Green to Walter T. Hudson, 8 Feb. 1951 (GP 635).

38. See U.S., Congress, Senate Foreign Relations Committee, *Hearings on Mutual Security Act of 1954*, 83d Cong., 2d sess., 4 June 1954, p. 19.

39. S. Doc. 27, *Report of Theodore Francis Green as a Delegate to the 7th General Assembly*, 83d Cong., 1st sess., 25 Feb. 1953, p. 13.

40. Green to Truman, 5 Jan. 1953; Thruston Morton to Green, 18 June 1953 (GP 713).

41. Green to John J. Cooney, 29 Aug. 1951 (GP 607).

42. Green to Horace H. Smith, 5 Aug. 1950 (GP 607).

43. See U.S., Congress, Senate Foreign Relations Subcommittee, *Hearings on United States Economic and Military Assistance to Free Europe*, 82d Cong., 1st sess., 7–23 July 1951.

44. *CR*, 31 Aug. 1951, pp. 10886–96.

45. Green to Stassen, 5 Nov. 1953; Stassen to Green, 5 Nov. 1953 (GP 702).

46. Speech at dedication of Touro Synagogue as a national shrine, Newport, R.I., 31 Aug. 1947 (GP 1045); Erwin L. Levine, *Theodore Francis Green: The Rhode Island Years, 1906–1936* (Providence, 1963), p. 200.

47. Memorandum, 13 Oct. 1938; Green to Roosevelt, 13 Oct. 1938 (GP 60).

48. Rabbi Stephen S. Wise to Green, 16 Oct. 1938; Green to Wise, 17 Oct. 1938 (GP 64). See also *CR*, app., 12 Jan. 1939, pp. 82–83. Grew to Green, 16 May 1945 (GP 370).

49. Green to Archibald Silverman, 2 Nov. 1945; Green to Connally, 7 Nov. 1945 (GP 370).

50. See S. Rept. 855 to accompany S. Con. Res. 44, 79th Cong., 1st sess., 12 Dec. 1945. See also *CR*, 17 Dec. 1945, pp. 12136–42, 12165–89, and 19 Dec. 1945, pp. 12381–96. See also Green to Harry S. Truman, 23 Oct. 1948 (GP 1124).

51. U.S. Congress, Senate Committees on Armed Services and Foreign Relations, *Hearings on Military Situation in the Far East*, 82d Cong., 1st sess., 1951, pp. 42–46.

52. Ibid., 924–25, 1401–3, 1541–42, 1652.

53. Ibid., pp. 3034–35.

54. See S.J. Res. 130, *CR*, 7 Feb. 1952, pp. 907–14.

55. Chafee to Green, 18 Feb. 1952 (GP 667); Wriston to Green, 12 Jan. 1954 (GP 758). *Providence Sunday Journal*, 30 Aug. 1953, sec. 3, p. 1.

56. *CR,* 26 Feb. 1954, p. 2374. It is interesting that Lyndon Johnson was not an opponent of the proposal, probably out of loyalty to the substitute's author, southerner Walter George.

57. Interview with Senator Bourke Hickenlooper of Iowa, 17 Jan. 1968.

58. Johnson to Higgins, 15 Dec. 1956 (GP 852).

59. Memorandum, n.d. (GP 1042).

60. Interview with Higgins.

61. *CR,* 12 June 1957, pp. 8937–38; *CR,* 28 May 1958, pp. 9733–34.

62. Green to John Foster Dulles, 31 Apr. 1957 (GP 876). *CR,* 8 May 1957, pp. 6542–85. Butler to Green, 10 May 1957 (GP 876).

63. Numerous letters were worded similarly and thus attested to an organized effort (GP 876).

64. S. Rept. 70, *Report of the Foreign Relations and Armed Services Committees on S.J. Res. 19,* 85th Cong., 1st sess., 14 Feb. 1957. Kennedy to Green, 27 Nov. 1956; Green to Lyndon B. Johnson, 10 Dec. 1956 (GP 898).

65. See S. Rept. 70, *Report of the Foreign Relations and Armed Services Committees on S.J. Res. 19,* 85th Cong., 1st sess., 14 Feb. 1957. See also *Congressional Quarterly,* 15 Feb. 1957, p. 199, and 18 Mar. 1957, p. 297.

66. *CR,* 19 Feb. 1957, pp. 2232–35; *CR,* 5 Mar. 1957, p. 3129; *CR,* 2 Apr. 1958, pp. 6073–74.

67. Interview with Higgins.

68. Press release, 12 Sept. 1958 (GP 923).

69. Dwight D. Eisenhower, *The White House Years, 1956–1961: Waging Peace* (Garden City, 1965), p. 301.

70. Press release, 12 Sept. 1958 (GP 923).

71. Green to Eisenhower, 29 Sept. 1958 (GP 923).

72. Eisenhower to Green, 2 Oct. 1958 (GP 923).

73. GP 923. The speech was given at a Democratic campaign dinner.

74. Press release, 27 Oct. 1958 (GP 923).

75. *Congressional Quarterly,* 14 Oct. 1960, p. 1721.

76. Interview with Higgins.

77. For attendance records, see GP 891.

78. S. Con. Res. 2, *CR,* 14 Jan. 1955, pp. 354–55; S. Con. Res. 101, *CR,* 15 July 1958, p. 13769; S. Res. 338, *CR,* 22 July 1958, p. 14538. Interview with Senator John Sparkman of Alabama, 10 May 1966; interview with Senator J. William Fulbright of Arkansas, 17 Jan. 1968.

79. This information was acquired from members of several committee staffs.

80. *Providence Journal,* 29 Jan. 1959, p. 17.

81. Green to Johnson, 29 Jan. 1959 (GP 959).

82. When Edward J. Higgins noticed that there were no representatives from the *Providence Journal* in the group of reporters, he slipped copies of the press release to Associated Press and United Press representatives, extracting promises that they would not call in the story until the meeting was over. Scooped through Higgins's quick thinking, the *Journal* received this announcement of such significance to its readers over press association wires. The paper's editorial on the resignation, which did not appear until 31 January (p. 13), commented that Green's decision could only "inspire a feeling of profound respect" and that, in the light of the seniority rule, "the only way to prevent members from clinging to such posts after the years had robbed them of their capacity to serve effectively is to appeal to their personal patriotism and moral courage."

Index